Post-Qualifying Child Care Social Work

Post-Qualifying Child Care Social Work

Developing Reflective Practice

Edited by
Gillian Ruch

Los Angeles • London • New Delhi • Singapore • Washington DC

SAGE Publications Ltd
1 Oliver's Yard
55 City Road
London EC1Y 1SP

SAGE Publications Inc.
2455 Teller Road
Thousand Oaks, California 91320

SAGE Publications India Pvt Ltd
B 1/I 1 Mohan Cooperative Industrial Area
Mathura Road
New Delhi 110 044

SAGE Publications Asia-Pacific Pte Ltd
33 Pekin Street #02-01
Far East Square
Singapore 048763

Library of Congress Control Number: 2008924219

British Library Cataloguing in Publication data

A catalogue record for this book is available from the British Library

ISBN 978-1-4129-2825-0
ISBN 978-1-4129-2826-7 (pbk)

Typeset by Cepha Imaging Pvt. Ltd., Bangalore, India
Printed in Great Britain by TJ International Ltd, Padstow, Cornwall
Printed on paper from sustainable resources

Mixed Sources
Product group from well-managed forests and other controlled sources
www.fsc.org   Cert no. SGS-COC-004704
© 1996 Forest Stewardship Council
FSC

Contents

Foreword

It is an honour to be invited to write a foreword to this book. Having spent almost 40 years of my professional life developing social work education and training, with particular reference to child welfare, I welcome the opportunity to comment on this collection of papers designed in response to the new post-qualification framework for social work with children and families (GSCC, 2005).

The aims, design and content of social work training have altered radically from the early days of the Charity Organisation Society. Over a century ago, the first social work course was set up at the London School of Economics as a series of evening lectures to inform, 'young ladies' engaged in voluntary work about the social sciences. By 2005, social work training had expanded, became clearer about knowledge, skills and values components and had an established qualification route within the university system. In the UK, aspiring social workers should undertake as a minimum qualification an undergraduate degree, followed by a range of post-qualification specialist courses, at the masters and doctorate levels. Additionally, social workers have recognised roles and tasks within the legal framework, in social policy and in the agencies for services delivery, both local authorities and voluntary sector organisations. Thus, from its early days of voluntary, philanthropic activity, social work has become recognised as a professional activity and a legally recognised career path. This is an impressive achievement.

It is inevitable and appropriate that social work has adjusted over time to societal, economic and political changes. Relevant education and training systems have been developed in response to these changing practices. While in many ways these changes have been necessary and appropriate, many academics and practitioners engaged in education and training have experienced them as happening too frequently and being overly reactive to criticism, particularly from the media. When organisations are under threat, they tend to adopt survival techniques, allowing changes to be made perhaps too hastily with insufficient attention to potential losses.

Applying these observations to specialist training in child care social work, it is clear that training has been buffeted from all sides by a range of processes. One of the most significant of these has been government responses to child deaths fuelled by the media. Major legislative and policy initiatives have been the direct result of an inquiry into a child death or criticisms of social work practice in risk assessment. The inquiry by Lord Laming into the death of Victoria Climbié (DoH, 2003) is the most recent example contributing significantly to the Every Child Matters agenda.

From the perspectives of social policy, political shifts away from universal approaches to social welfare have had a profound impact on social work with families. Thatcherism, characterised by emphasising non-intervention, self-reliance and new managerialism, led to the introduction of standardised frameworks for assessment. Although these have the advantage of making professional activity more transparent and therefore more accountable, there are real dangers, that practice has become mechanistic and that training requirements have gradually adjusted in response. Training has become more structured, too heavily dependent on competence indicators and overly reliant on the 'what works' agenda' in research.

Lower priority seems to have been given to capacity for reflection in education and training structures. This must remain a crucial element within training at all levels because of the unique nature of the circumstances involving social work activity. Throughout history, it has been essential for social workers to reflect before they respond to the most complex and often painful circumstances requiring their intervention. It is the strength of this edited book that the reflection process is drawn back to the centre of the social work training arena alongside observational and collaborative practice, aspects of the work underpinning all interventions. Capacities to observe, reflect and to collaborate should take root at the undergraduate level and be nurtured, so that they flower and infuse all post-qualification initiatives.

A further strength of this book is its being aware of the need to listen to service users and also to the voices of students. Theirs is the direct proof that these themes of reflection and observation play a critical part in professional learning. The vivid illustrations provided by students enrich the chapters prepared by their very experienced teachers who have contributed to this volume.

Future students of post-qualifying social work training courses specialising in child care will find this volume a valuable companion to their studies. In the 'evening phase' of my career, it inspires me with hope that the things I have always held essential to practice have not been lost. No training courses can be static, but should be responsive to current and future professional demands, building on existing strengths derived from decades of evolution. The editor and contributors deserve praise for the quality and content of each of the chapters and for the effective marrying of unique student experience with established research and literature.

Dr. Gillian Bridge
Former Senior Lecturer in the Department of Social Policy at the London School of Economics
and External Examiner for the Wessex Post-Qualification Child Care Award

Part One

The contemporary framework of post-qualification child care practice

Chapter 1

Introduction – developing holistic social work practitioners

Gillian Ruch

The introduction of the new post-qualification (PQ) framework for social work with children and families (GSCC, 2005) has come at a time when, within the field of childcare social work, there is a growing body of evidence that emphasises the importance for service users and carers of relationships with social workers that are sustained, inclusive and honest (Bell, 2002; De Boer and Coady, 2007; Munro, 2001). The importance of effective professional relationships was reinforced for the social work academics responsible for this book, when they consulted with service users and carers in the design and content of the PQ curriculum that informs this book. The incident is recorded in more detail in Chapter 9, but suffice it to say the main priority of this group of stakeholders was the ability for practitioners to be able to sustain a committed and effective relationship with them in the face of ever-increasing organisational expectations and the emotional demands of the work.

This book aims to equip practitioners with the skills, knowledge and value base to realise the aspirations expressed by these service users and carers. To achieve these aims, however, it is necessary to be clear about the nature of the obstacles that might get in the way and to be able to articulate key professional practice and pedagogic principles that will assist in their attainment.

The challenge of contemporary childcare social work

What are the key challenges facing childcare social workers practicing today? Words that immediately spring to mind are risk, regulation, the 'blame culture', managerialism, the marketisation of welfare, competence, reflective practice, inter-professional working, collaboration, professionalism, diversity and difference, service user and carer perspectives and evidence-based practice. In a nutshell a *competent, evidence-based* childcare social worker needs to practice *reflectively* and *collaboratively*, within a *regulatory, managerialistic, resource-led, inter-professional work* context, that recognises *diversity and difference* and actively seeks to understand and respond to this through encouraging *service users and carers* to articulate their views. Put in this way it immediately becomes apparent that not only is childcare social work challenging, it is full of tensions, with potentially competing demands being placed simultaneously on practitioners. Identifying the issues inevitably raises some tricky questions:

- How can practitioners be helped to practice effectively and reflectively, in order to resist the managerial imperatives that reduce the professional social work role to a narrowly defined bureaucrat?
- What knowledge, skills and values do practitioners need to feel confident about taking risks in partnership with service users and carers?
- How can the inhibiting effects of the blame culture surrounding social work practice be minimised?

This book seeks, in partnership with its readers, to think about and respond to these complex questions.

Background to the book

The idea for the book arose out of discussions amongst childcare social work academics and experienced practitioners who were responsible for developing a new PQ programme. The challenge of designing and delivering the new PQ curriculum in many respects mirrored the challenges of practice. The PQ education context, like practice contexts, embraces a broad range of stakeholders including service users and carers, social work academics, the Department of Health, GSCC and employer agencies. Identifying and responding to the diverse expectations of these different groupings proved an enormous task and required the curriculum development team to devise a programme that could cover a breadth and depth of skills and knowledge for qualified childcare social work practitioners in tight timescales.

How then did we endeavour to remain, to use a phrase central to Chapter 10, creative and innovative, within a regulated, prescriptive and demanding curriculum framework? First, we identified three core principles which we believe are fundamental to effective and ethical childcare social work practice and which address the GSCC PQ standards and requirements (GSCC, 2005). These three principles are:

- Reflective practice
- Observational practice
- Collaborative practice

In the book these principles are evident in two ways: in the discrete chapters bearing their names in Sections One and Two; and as themes, particularly in the case of reflective practice, that are woven into several of the chapters in Section Two.

Secondly, the importance of promoting the integration of theory and practice and making the curriculum demands of the programme relevant for busy practitioners has been addressed by candidates being encouraged to bring their own practice experiences, challenges and dilemmas into the classroom discussions. In the practice arena the role of the practice assessor has been to help practitioners to relate classroom-based learning to their practice contexts. A closer integration of academic and practice-based assignments has also been introduced to reinforce the importance of the theory–practice relationship. The structure of this book has aimed to achieve a similar integration of theory and practice, with material inspired or written by candidates woven in different ways and to differing degrees, into the chapters. Chapter 8, for example, includes candidates' comments about the contribution of their child observation experiences to their professional development and practice, whilst Chapter 9 has examples of candidates 'in the classroom' exploring new practice skills.

Thirdly, in keeping with the PQ requirements for self-directed learning, the Programme embraces facilitated learning in small groups (action learning sets) and dialogical pedagogic approaches. Dialogue is encouraged in the book in two ways:

- Chapters include reflective activities to assist the reader in applying the ideas to their own practice context.
- Chapters end with a series of reflective questions to encourage the reader to think further about what they have learnt and to develop their reflective awareness.

The structure of the book

The book is divided into two sections. Section One comprises six chapters, three of which introduce the key principles (referred to above) underpinning the PQ programme from which the book originated. The remaining three chapters address the core teaching and learning requirements generic to all PQ programmes regardless of specialism – the consolidation unit (Chapter 2) with its emphasis on self-directed learning and the practice education unit (Chapter 6), which equips practitioners to develop assessment and support skills in relation to colleagues and students. In Section Two the chapters focus on the five modules taught on the PQ programme and explore the integration of theory and practice in relation to: child development, child observation, working in partnership with children, the challenges of regulatory practice contexts and collaborative, and inter-professional working.

In the opening section of the book, Chapter 2 by Tunney discusses the requirements underpinning and the principles of the consolidation unit on PQ programmes. Against the backdrop of the recent changes in the PQ framework Tunney highlights how maximising the benefits for practitioners of PQ programmes and CPD requires the educational institutions and employing bodies to have shared understanding of the nature of PQ training. She suggests that the existence of such an integrated approach can be demonstrated by PQ candidates in the learning contracts that they are required to complete, through self-directed activities and action learning sets. The importance of candidates experiencing themselves and their employers as belonging to a 'learning organisation', that is supportive of PQ candidates and understanding of the demands PQ programmes make on candidates, is crucial to their PQ experience.

Chapter 3 explores one of the three fundamental principles on which the PQ programme is founded – reflective practice. In this chapter Ruch underlines the anxiety-ridden nature of contemporary childcare social work and the central role played by reflective practice in addressing the anxiety-related obstacles to effective practice. The chapter goes on to explore understandings of reflective practice but cautions that, whilst widely acknowledged as an important component of effective practice, how reflective practice is operationalised and the conditions required for it to flourish are less familiar to practitioners and managers. Drawing on the concepts of emotional literacy and the learning organisation the chapter concludes with what Ruch considers to be the core characteristics of reflective forums for the promotion of reflective practice.

Observational skills in and for social work practice are the focus of Chapter 4. In this chapter, Ruch outlines the key features of the Tavistock Model of child observation, highlighting how the whole process, from identifying a child to observing through to presenting an observation recording to a seminar group, is rich with learning opportunities. Particular attention is paid to the dynamics of mirroring and containment, both important features of the seminar groups, that contribute to candidates learning. The richness of the learning gained from the observation experience is explored in more detail in Chapter 8.

Chapter 5, which is complemented by Chapter 11, introduces the reader to the emergent contours of inter-professional practice and the government-driven Every Child Matters agenda with its associated programmes and priorities. This policy context provides the backdrop to a more detailed exploration in Chapter 11 of the challenges it poses for collaborative, inter-professional working.

The final chapter in Section One explores the new requirements for all practitioners to acquire practice education skills. In this chapter Bhatti-Sinclair explores the challenges facing PQ programmes, employers and practitioners due to the reconfiguration of practice education. One of the biggest challenges relates to the diminution of the practice teacher role to one of practice assessor and the potential undervaluing and inadequate resourcing of practice education within agency settings. Despite these challenges the *Enabling Others* unit, core to all specialist level PQ programmes, has the potential to offer PQ candidates a sound foundation in supervision, mentoring and assessment skills.

Given the powerful constraints on contemporary childcare practice, which are largely government-driven, it might appear more logical to begin Section Two with a chapter examining current contexts for practice (Chapter 10). Instead, in keeping with our commitment to child-centred practice, the section begins with two chapters (7 and 8) that provide a close-up exploration of children and child development. In the subsequent chapter (Chapter 9) the focus widens to embrace the broader social context of children before the section concludes with two chapters (10 and 11) that address the professional contexts of contemporary practice.

In Chapter 7, Gully invites the reader to think about children from four perspectives – the physical, psychological, parented and social child – and suggests that all of these perspectives impact on how social workers understand and engage with children. An important implication of this approach is the emphasis it places on the influence of wider socio-political factors on the construction of children and childhood and on professional responses to children in general and those with additional and complex needs, in particular.

Chapter 8 on child observation builds on Chapter 4 in Section One but this time from the perspective of practitioner learning and the contribution of the observation experience to professional development. In this chapter, McKinnon makes a strong argument for the value of focussing on the 'normal' child as a way of developing advanced skills and understanding of children with more challenging needs. Once again, in line with Chapter 7, a significant feature of the learning acquired by practitioners engaging in observation is their heightened understanding, not only of the needs of individual children but the wider impact on their development and well-being of the socio-political context in which they are growing up.

In Chapter 9, Ruch focuses on the skills and knowledge needed for effective partnership working with children, young people, their families and carers. The chapter has a particular skills orientation and introduces the reader to two systemic approaches – sculpting and reflective conversations – that equip practitioners to develop partnerships with families and to engage with them in inclusive and potentially empowering ways. The second half of the chapter considers the role and importance of focussed therapeutic work with children and provides suggestions for undertaking meaningful practice outcome evaluations.

Chapter 10 examines some of the biggest challenges facing childcare social workers in their efforts to avoid being reduced to 'bureau-professionals'. Against the backdrop of child-centred and relationship-based partnership practice, Rogers explores the challenges of remaining innovative and creative in practice, in the context of pervasive and ever-changing bureaucratic requirements. The significance of the risk society and its impact on regulatory frameworks, managerialism, surveillance and supervision and what is valued as evidence for practice are all examined. The chapter concludes with recommendations for how creativity and innovation can be sustained in what can be experienced as a hostile climate for professional practice.

In the penultimate chapter in the book, Chapter 11, Warren-Adamson connects the ideas about inter-professional working introduced in Chapter 5 and relates them to the rapidly developing inter-professional context of contemporary childcare practice. Whilst not a new phenomenon, inter-professional working has taken on a new meaning post-Climbié with the Government's Every Child Matters agenda and the requirement that all children's services be integrated into Children's Trusts by 2008. This chapter introduces a rich mix of theoretical frameworks – ideas about collaboration, complexity, systems, formality and informality, cultures of care, intervention and theories of change, sites for practice and group processes – which encourage engagement with the challenges of collaborative and inter-professional working practice.

Chapter 12 concludes the book by identifying how practitioners can be encouraged to keep their professional development as a continuous process through dynamic relationships with themselves, with service users, with their managers and with the socio-political context in which they practice.

Moving forward and continuing professional development

Each chapter stands in its own right but also given the philosophy underpinning the programme design there is considerable overlap between chapters. The intention of the book overall is to encourage practitioners to develop their reflective responses to practice on all levels – the personal, professional and political and the individual, organisational and societal. These holistic approaches to practice are the essence of effective and reflective practice and it is our hope that such an holistic professional identity is the aspiration of all PQ candidates.

Chapter 2

The PQ framework, PQ and CPD developments: consolidation unit

Gill Tunney

Chapter learning aims

- To explore notions of the profession – current challenges to the profession – and the recognition that social work is a profession that is contingent on context
- To examine the development of the new post-qualifying (PQ) framework and the place of the consolidation unit within the Children and Families post-qualification award
- To analyse the place of the PQ awards within the context of continuous professional development emphasizing the importance of the learning organisation and situating the learner within an appropriately supportive environment
- To introduce the concepts of Self-Managed Learning (SML) approaches to PQ awards generally and the consolidation unit in particular

Introduction: social work as a profession that is contingent on context

Social work has always been a turbulent profession. In search of a coherent professional identity, debates have raged over establishing whether the profession has a sound foundation for 'generic' practice or for the development of 'specialisation' (Stevenson, 2005). The idea that social work has a core of values, knowledge and skills that can be applied to any situation forms the basis of establishing a social work qualification (the new social work degree) that is designed on generic principles, supplemented by a suite of specialist PQ awards.

However, early debates within the profession were not only concerned with genericism versus specialisation but were also polarised between those, on the one hand, who believed that structural problems within society should be dealt with thus alleviating the poverty and other factors at community level that lead to social exclusion and, on the other, those who felt that social workers should focus on individual case work – finding ways to improve the well-being of the service user. This dichotomy has been described as the 'community work' and 'casework' approaches (Stevenson, 2005). These approaches, often driven by different value bases, can characterise how social workers think and act. Indeed there is some evidence that social workers can combine the operation of a welfare agenda with individual therapeutic approaches and value the use of these skills as empowerment mechanisms (Woodcock and Dixon, 2005). More recent arguments include the recognition of the institutional context of social work, and the importance of 'contextually created difference' (McDonald *et al.*, 2003:191). As a result the identity of social work can become diffused with that of other occupational groups in multi-disciplinary teams, as organisations respond to 'mixed economies' of service delivery (McDonald *et al.*, 2003:203), and the host service becomes the new context. Thus, the social work profession can be difficult to define – it can depend on the context of the job, the approach of the individual social worker and the professional identity they may have; it can also depend on the multi-sectoral nature of the service provision and the relevant quality framework for measuring service outcomes.

Other factors which have contributed to the turbulence within the profession include organisational restructuring, political and societal imperatives and the emergence of evidence-based performance measurement across the public sector. One of the results of reorganisation has been the emergence of specialist departments in the statutory sector and service-user-group-oriented voluntary services. Both sectors are subject to increasing bureaucratisation and managerialism that results in the profession (in any context) having to respond to criterion-referenced performance measures (Adams, 2002). These imperatives result from a change in governance that attempts to drive up service performance in response to perceived failures in the past. For instance one of the most influential of all pressures in the field has been the impact of child protection inquiries (Stevenson, 2005). These and other pressures have fuelled the move towards increased partnership working, inter- and multi-professional working and the breaking down of professional boundaries.

A newly qualified social worker, therefore, might emerge from the social work degree with a firm grounding in a set of generic principles (based on a set of published competencies, for instance the National Occupational Standards), including values, knowledge and skills relating to social work practice. However, it is likely that, even before qualifying, learners will have demonstrated their competence in a specialist setting, as there are very few 'generic' practice learning opportunities. These settings are increasingly inter- or multi-professional and based in non-traditional settings. They may have already encountered the fact that professional social work practice can be variable in its manifestation, depending on the legal context and the setting in which social work is practiced.

So, in practice, many social workers find themselves, once qualified, in a very broad range of different contexts, perhaps working alongside other qualified social workers, or other social care professionals such as health care, criminal justice, education or housing professionals. Even within the specialist area of children and families, newly qualified workers could find themselves in one of a range of different settings depending on whether the post was situated in, say, adoption, disabled children, family support and child protection, fostering, initial response teams, looking after children or outreach work – all of which sit within the statutory sector. In addition there are increasingly a range of positions that are filled by social workers in voluntary and other agencies such as SureStart and CAFCAS, all of which could present differing professional demands on a newly qualified worker.

Reflective Activity[1]

Where have you been?

- When did you qualify?
- What sort of course was it?
- What sort of practice settings have you experienced?
- Can you describe your own professional identity?
- Can you describe your own framework of values?
- What kinds of inter-professional experience have you had?
- How much can you already demonstrate against the qualifying standards?
- Did you have any outstanding learning needs?

The development of the new post-qualifying framework

There have, for some time, been specialist training and development opportunities for those working in specialist settings and, since 1990, the PQ framework has been developed, originally by CCETSW and more recently by the General Social Care Council (GSCC).

> The framework was conceived as a structure for the continuous professional development of qualified social workers with four, related, aims:
>
> - To formally recognise the professional development of qualified social workers
> - To ensure common minimum standards across a wide variety of post-qualifying education and training, in different sectors and settings
> - To promote education, training and qualifications for social workers that support high standards of service and care in the personal social services
> - To provide structures for post-qualifying education and training that are flexible and responsive to the changing needs of service delivery and changing career pathways
>
> (GSCC, 2001)

In 1997, the PQ framework was reviewed and whilst retaining the framework structure of the award – it established two levels of achievement – the PQSW (Post-Qualifying award in Social Work) at Honours degree level, and the AASW (Advanced Award in Social Work) at Masters Level. Learners could make their way through six PQ awards – PQ1 which was a generic consolidation of practice award and was a condition of entry to further parts of the award structure; PQ2-4 which could be generic or specialist, and focussed on complex situations, risk management and decision making; and the Practice Teacher Award which encompassed both PQ5 – networks and multi-disciplinary aspects; and PQ6 – competence in enabling others.

There were, therefore, post-qualifying awards designed for particular settings such as the PQCCA (Post-Qualifying Child Care Award), which was mapped onto the requirements for the PQSW. Similar awards also existed for Mental Health, Practice Teaching and the Regulation of Care Services, for instance. These awards have been delivered by PQ consortia across the country made up of at least one Higher Education provider and one social services provider – such consortia have developed many useful collaborative arrangements to deliver innovative programmes.

A comprehensive review of the PQ framework was again commenced in 2002, and following wide consultation, the new framework was launched in 2005, with a few programmes commencing in 2006 (Early Start programmes), the remainder to start in 2007. The consultation exercise revealed the following perceived weaknesses about the existing framework:

> Responses on identified weaknesses fell into four main clusters; the complexity of the framework and varia-tion in standards; the bureaucracy of the system; problems with resourcing, including the availability of assessors and mentors; and problems with implementation and ownership by employers. Comments were also made about the lack of evaluation of PQ generally.
>
> (GSCC, 2003)

Following further consultation in 2004, the new framework was developed incorporating the feedback and includes:

- The integration of professional development with the development of the workforce
- The meeting of both generic and specialist requirements
- The linking of supervision, appraisal and performance management to key stages of professional development
- The recognition that at the post-qualifying level social work practice becomes increasingly diverse
- The development of strong inter-professional links enabling social workers to study alongside other professions
- Raising standards of practice – emphasizing the role of workplace learning and clearly stating how practice competence will be assessed
- Fully integrated academic and professional learning

(GSCC, 2005)

The new PQ framework is based on three levels:

Specialist: consolidating, extending and deepening professional competence in a specialist context – likely to be delivered at Honours level

Higher Specialist: focusing on the knowledge and skills necessary to make complex judgements and discharge high levels of responsibility for the co-ordination of social support and the management of risk – to be delivered at post-graduate diploma level

Advanced: focusing on the knowledge and skills required for professional leadership and the improvement of services – to be delivered at Masters level

(GSCC, 2005)

The conceptual model underlying the revised PQ framework is based on three principles:

- That some standards underpin social work at all levels and should be integral to both the qualifying degree and PQ programmes
- That the process of continuing professional development can be seen in terms of *levels* of professional development common to all: specialist, higher specialist and advanced as described above
- That professional competence beyond the point of qualification and in a specialist context can only be meaningfully evaluated against national standards associated with a *specialist* area of practice

(GSCC, 2005)

The GSCC have produced Specialist Standards to be met by post-qualifying awards in education and training in social work in a range of areas. These are:

- Children and Young People, their Families and Carers
- Social Work with Adults
- Mental Health
- Practice Education (at Higher Specialist and Advanced levels only)
- Leadership and Management

All awards at specialist level have to include the consolidation of practice in a specialist setting, enabling the development of others, and inter-professional practice. This chapter focuses on the broad principles of the consolidation unit as an integral component of all the PQ specialist streams but invites the reader to apply it to their specific childcare social work settings.

Reflective Activity

Where are you now?

- Where do you work?
- What kind of team do you work in?
- What is your specialism?
- What kinds of inter-professional working are there?
- What do you already know about the specialist context?
- What do you already know about the specialist award?
- Do any of your co-workers hold a PQ qualification?

The place of the PQ awards within the context of continuous professional development

A handbook published by the GSCC in 2001 for PQ training and education emphasised the importance of integrating the PQ framework into agencies' management processes – in particular arrangements for inducting new staff into the specialist context, continuous professional development of staff throughout their careers, progression through career scales, and improvements on service outcomes (GSCC, 2001).

However evidence from some consortia suggests that these development and training initiatives can have a limited impact on service effectiveness. It has been suggested (Skinner and Whyte, 2004) that only a commitment to the principles of a learning organisation, in which the agency is fully involved with supporting the learner in order to achieve transformational change and continuous improvement, can ensure effective professional development. They suggest that 'a culture of curiosity and of learning needs to be established and maintained if staff are to be nourished and supported in taking the risks involved' (Skinner and Whyte, 2004:376). In a learning organisation, staff are encouraged to be self-critical, to examine working practices within a supportive environment, and to encourage reflective practice against internal and external benchmarks. The emphasis here is on support – so that the learner has the confidence to question without fear of criticism, and to be comfortable enough to be self-critical.

Other findings provide evidence of a more direct link between performance and training – 'an increase in confidence in their understanding of and ability to carry out the professional role' was reported by a small-scale study carried by the Top South West PQ consortium (Mitchell, 2001:436). The study also reported impacts on practice in three areas:

- Increased knowledge and understanding of theory
- Developing more effective communication
- Increased understanding of process and political issues

The study reported that 'the most effective impact was where there were good links between operational managers and training, involving managers at all levels and operating through a negotiated infrastructure which provided the necessary support and assessment systems' (2001:438).

However these impacts were variable across and within agencies. The most positive impacts occurred where learners were encouraged to take on responsibility for others or for reviewing and implementing new policies or practices. 'Impact on practice was greatest when learning was an integrated part of work' (2001:441). Conversely, the most negative impacts were experienced within organisations whose cultures were not conducive to continuous professional development, or that were suffering from reorganisations, staff shortages and inequitable access to development opportunities. 'The importance of first line managers as arbiters of practice was borne out in this study' (2001:440).

One definition of continuous professional development is being 'concerned with development of flexible knowledge and transferable skills capable of adaptation within fast changing contexts and requirements of the working environment' (Postle et al., 2002:159). The challenge for the development of new PQ programmes is how to integrate the development of these knowledge and skills into the practice environment, and how to evidence them to meet academic levels and standards. Agencies involved in consortia programmes want to be able to measure outcomes, whereas educators are interested in the process of learning. It is argued that it is not possible to focus just on the outcomes (typically measured by evidence against competences, driven by service imperatives or improvements) or on the process of learning (typically measured by reflective journals or academic assessment), but that a preferable approach would be to see development as a continuous process that could be measured over time (Postle *et al.*, 2002). This process must be embedded in agencies' approaches to recruitment, induction, appraisal and retention of staff – continuous professional development based on reflective practice, in order to continuously improve services to the children, young people and their families who use them.

Reflective Activity

Where do you want to get to?

- What was your induction programme like?
- Have you completed your probationary period?
- Have these identified any learning goals (training and development needs?)
- What support is there for continuous professional development in your organisation?
- How would you describe your organisational culture?
- Are there any things in your or others' practice that you would like to change?
- What feedback have you, your team or organisation had from those who use your services?

The learning contract and self-managed learning – how to integrate theory and practice

Just as those who use services must be at the heart of reviewing and developing service provision, so must the learner and their workplace be at the heart of reviewing and developing their own practice within any post-qualifying programme. Sobiechowska and Maisch (2006) classify this type of work-based learning as:

> *work-based learning where students are full-time employees whose programme of study is embedded in the workplace and is designed to meet the learning needs of the employees and the aims of the organisation*
>
> (2006:270).

Boud and Solomon (2001) describe work-based learning as having the following characteristics:

- A partnership, maybe contractual, between an external organisation and an educational institution specifically established to foster learning
- A programme derived from the needs of the workplace – work is the curriculum- established once learners have identified their current competencies and learning
- Learning projects oriented to the challenges of work and the future needs of learner and organisation
- The assessment of learning outcomes under the auspices of an educational institution and with respect to a framework of standards and levels

(cited in Sobiechowska and Maisch, 2006:270)

These characteristics describe the approach to post-qualifying awards in social work and the new framework in particular, which are to be employer-led and linked to agencies induction and continuous professional development frameworks. The consolidation unit, in particular, within the new PQ framework can provide the learner with a structured introduction to the award, and place the learner and their practice at the centre. Building on the existing strengths of the PQ1, the unit will enable the learner to develop the skills necessary to review their own competencies, research the necessary standards, enquire reflectively into their own practice and demonstrate expertise to a level satisfactory for both academic achievement and their agency's own requirements. By being placed at the start of the award, the unit provides a sound beginning to their development through the new qualification, which will inevitably mean better outcomes from the learning overall and will be an essential foundation for effective child care practice based on sound principles.

At the heart of the consolidation unit is the requirement to demonstrate competence in the specialist context. Here is the key to an approach based on SML. The many contexts that social workers work in, referred to above, and the range of different situations that children, young people and families present as well as differing service-user and carer groups, are likely to have a myriad of requirements and standards specific to the specialist context and organisation. Within a Self-managed Learning approach (Cunningham *et al.*, 2000) the learner can bring this context to each award, by setting their learning within a structured and negotiated Learning Contract, and evaluating their progress against this, supported by tutor input and peer learning groups.

Self-managed learning can allow the learner to gain benefit from and credit for all the informal types of learning that occur within the workplace. These can include the induction and probationary processes already mentioned but include reflecting on learning from colleagues, reflecting on own practice, through engagement with those who use services, and can also include the acquisition of knowledge and skills under the supervision of a more experienced practitioner (Bennett, 2000). Depending on the aspirations of the individual learner, the contract can also include the learner's own personal development goals, thus allowing learners to place their learning within a particular context into the broader one of their own lifelong learning. By focussing on learning rather than education, an SML approach can develop a range of transferable skills in workers who will be able to demonstrate the sort of autonomy and independence that underpins good evidence-based practice.

This approach is not new and has been evidenced and evaluated by many post qualifying programme across various professions and can pose some challenges (Sobiechowska and Maisch, 2006; Morgan, Rawlinson and Weaver, 2006; Williams, 2001; Looi Chng and Coombs, 2006). The difficulties that such an approach can present to tutors and learners can include: the length of time learners take to draft a learning contract; the lack of support from learners and their sponsoring organisations in relation to peer group meetings; and verifying evidence and introducing rigour into material drawn from the workplace.

These challenges can be overcome, however, with a sufficiently structured approach to self-managed learning. The placing of the SML process within a PQ specialist award determines the framework for the learning goals to some extent. The programme can structure the steps that the learners take in order to construct a meaningful learning contract. Tutors can present relevant learning materials to facilitate the understanding of specialist areas of knowledge and understanding. Mentors can help learners move forward through the process. Above all, the establishment of a peer learning group provides the forum for the development of goals and sharing of practice that enables reflective learning to take place. Tutor-facilitated groups can ensure that important deadlines are met, and give formative feedback on learning contracts. By placing these within a theoretical context of evidence-based practice and requiring candidates to carry out developmental tasks and evaluate these, the consolidation unit can provide an essential foundation for not only the further study on the PQ award, but also for continuous professional development in the agency context (Rutter, 2006). It can, therefore, provide a set of underpinning principles for the learner, essential to their continuous professional development – those of reflective practice, collaborative working, observational skills and the integration of theory and practice.

Reflective Activity

How will you get there?

- What 'gaps' in your learning or competence have you identified so far?
- What action could you take to progress from where you are to where you would like to be?
- What action would your service-users/line manager/organisation like you to take?
- What learning do you need to undertake in order to be able to do these things?
- How do these fit in with your personal goals, your professional aspirations?
- What resources do you need (access to knowledge, people, time)?

Through a self-managed learning group, learners can negotiate a Learning Contract that itself can become evidence for the achievement of learning outcomes. A contract should identify the context and standards against which the learner has assessed their competence. Evidence has to be presented demonstrating competence and identifying gaps and learning needs. A strategy has to be developed to meet the learning needs identified and this strategy has to be evaluated. Part of this will be an assessment of whether the learning needs have been met by the actions identified. At least some of these will be aligned with the programme and short-term enough to be evaluated. One of the benefits of learners negotiating their own contracts is the added value of self- and peer assessment. Learners have to present their case for the achievement of their learning goals and peers will examine these critically (Dawes, 2000). This activity in itself develops the critical self-reflection skills so necessary in the profession. For instance self-managed peer learning groups can provide the support necessary to discuss and resolve some of the challenges currently facing child care workers, such as the consequences of audit and performance measurement, the promotion of relationship-based social work and the wider role social workers have in preventative and protection services for children (Gupta and Blewett, 2007).

Reflective Activity

How will you know when you get there?

- What evidence will you be able to provide that you are competent in the specialist context?
- How will you demonstrate the achievement of your learning goals?
- How will you measure your achievement?
- How can you verify your workplace evidence?
- How can you assess your workplace practice?
- Will you be able to obtain feedback on improving your practice from those who use services?

A self-managed learning contract approach allows the learner to bring their specialist context and relate their learning to particular service-user groups or areas of professional interest. The first stage would be for the learner to locate themselves within the appropriate professional context; then to identify the appropriate range of standards and competencies required for that particular role; then to demonstrate competence with evidence against relevant standards identifying any gaps; these gaps and other personal and professional learning goals form the learning contract. The learner is then required to develop strategies to meet their learning goals, to implement these and to evaluate the evidence within the context of a peer learning group. This approach could be used not only to meet the requirements of the consolidation unit, but also as a basis for supporting learning throughout the PQ award.

The learner thus develops a most important transferable skill – that of locating oneself within a professional role and identifying strategies for continuous development. It also underpins the development of reflective practice placing an emphasis on how this is both an individual and a collective, collaborative activity (see Chapter 3). These are the same skills that are increasingly needed for effective service review and self-critical practice. This 'deep' and transferable learning and the potential of self-managed learning is perhaps best captured by the experience and comments of one PQ candidate:

> My learning in this unit has exceeded my expectation and I put this down largely to the action learning sets and the way that they encouraged a deeper level of reflection than I would usually enter into. The experience of analysing my role in the context of performance monitoring has highlighted an almost complete absence of this approach. This in turn has demonstrated to me that I am responsible for my own development and learning in a way I don't think I had previously fully comprehended.

> The key area of this particular experience came as a consequence of studying alongside social workers who are more accustomed to reflective practice in their everyday occupation. The discussions held with my fellow students led me to think long and hard about how we know that what we are doing is what we should be doing in the way we should be doing it.

Chapter summary

- Social work is a profession that is contingent on context; these contexts are becoming increasingly diverse and often include inter- or multi-professional working; hence education providers are unlikely to be able to respond to all these different contexts within a taught curriculum.
- The new PQ framework provides an opportunity to devise programmes which situate the learner within their own context through a process of learning which links to CPD structures within agencies.
- Service-user-centred practice can be at the heart of the learning where practitioners can situate their learning within their particular context; work-based learning provides an opportunity to enable learners to be independent and autonomous by devising their own learning contracts, relevant to their agency setting and particular service-user group.
- The consolidation unit provides the basis for the learning contract which can be negotiated and supported through self-managed or peer-managed action learning sets.

Reflective questions

From reading this chapter, what have you learnt about the CPD requirements of the social work profession and the principles underpinning PQ training that you were previously unaware of?

Which aspect of the PQ training process interests you most?

Which aspect of the self-directed learning do you think you will find most difficult and how might you address this?

Note

1. *The five questions posed to learners in this chapter are taken from the Self-managed Learning approach outlined by Cunningham, Bennett and Dawes (2000).*

Chapter 3

Reflective practice and reflective spaces

Gillian Ruch

Chapter learning aims

- To provide an awareness of the contribution of reflective practice to ethically informed and effective practice
- To develop practitioners' understanding of the different types of reflective practice
- To outline individual and collaborative support mechanisms and the necessary personal qualities and organisational conditions that promote and sustain reflective practice

Introduction: the emergence of reflective practice

Over the past 15 years, the term 'reflective practitioner' has crept into social work education and practice. The gradual absorption of the notion of the reflective practitioner into mainstream social work practice has been accompanied by an assumption that everyone knows what being a reflective practitioner involves and how becoming a reflective practitioner is facilitated and realised. The substantial literature that explores the differing views on what constitutes reflective practice clearly illustrates this is not the case and highlights the existence of a conceptual minefield (Ixer, 1999, 2000; Quinn, 2000). Conversely, it is the dearth of literature on how reflective practice can be promoted, that renders understandings of reflective practice, and the identification of the conditions required for its development, problematic.

This chapter seeks to explore the challenging and contested ideas that surround reflective practice by:

- Identifying why reflective practice is important and its contribution to the prevailing evidence-based agendas and debates
- Outlining the key characteristics of reflective practice alongside some of its contested aspects

- Focussing on the individual traits and organisational contexts that facilitate the development of reflective practitioners through the creation of reflective spaces

In so doing the chapter meets one of the key requirements of the post-qualification professional development framework, which requires social workers to use reflection and critical analysis to develop and improve their practice.

Why is reflective practice important?

Perhaps the first and most important question to ask at the outset of this chapter is why is reflective practice important? To answer this question it is necessary to explore the nature of knowledge(s) informing social work practice and the current emphasis on evidence-based practice.

'Knowledges' in social work practice

Up until relatively recently, social work, along with other professions operating in conditions of modernity, have been premised on the belief that scientific understandings of the world are the most reliable and desirable. Scientific understandings of knowledge sometimes referred to as modernist or positivist understandings, claim that an objective body of knowledge exists and that there is a 'truth' to be discovered. Scientific endeavours seek to identify causal relationships that are claimed as the 'truth'. From this perspective, knowledge is of a technical–rational nature, i.e. there is an explanation for why something happens and a particular response that will address it. In the case of social work practice such an understanding would mean that specific factors could be identified as contributing to the incidence of child abuse. The removal of these conditions would reduce, or even eliminate, as some positivistic thinkers would claim, the occurrence of child abuse. This approach fails to recognise the complexity of the 'knowledges' informing professional practice in inter-personal contexts.

Positivist understandings of knowledge have dominated thinking in modern times. Priority has been placed on scientific testing to 'prove' that something is 'true'. The evidence-based practice agendas currently influencing 'best practice' are closely related to this tradition of scientific knowledge and privilege certain forms of evidence, e.g. research evidence derived from randomised controlled trials, over other 'less scientific' sources of evidence. The challenge for the social work profession and discipline is to assert the limitations of scientific perspectives on knowledge, given social work's roots in the social sciences and its focus of attention on human beings and behaviours. In contrast and of greater relevance to social work practice are post-modern understandings of knowledge that emphasise:

- First, a belief that phenomena are socially constructed and that every human encounter is unique
- Secondly, a disbelief in objectivity and a commitment to subjectivity as an inevitable, unavoidable and necessary component of understanding
- Thirdly, the value-laden enterprise of knowledge generation

From this perspective there is not a single objective truth but multiple inter-subjective truths constructed through human encounters. It is this understanding of 'knowledges' and truths that underpins the concept of reflective practice. Multiple sources of knowledge are of particular importance in reflective practice as practitioners are not simply drawing on rational, cognitive knowledge but irrational, affective knowledge or, put more simply, emotional feelings as well as cognitive facts. According to Gould (1996), reflective practice is an inclusive, umbrella term that involves acquiring professional knowledge through the systematic examination of experiences encountered in practice. In addition to conventional knowledge sources such as research and theories, reflective practice embraces, '*practice skills, human judgement, artistry, intuition and tacit knowledge*' (Gould, 1996:4), and has as a key characteristic the ability to transcend hierarchies and dichotomies, for example between fact and feeling, rational and emotional, researcher and practitioner. By engaging with a diverse range of knowledge sources practitioners develop a holistic understanding of themselves, their clients and their practice. Consequently practitioners develop into reflectively, rather than technically, competent professionals. Reflective practice enables practitioners to theorise their practice by drawing on knowledge embedded in practice (Fisher and Somerton, 1997) and to practice theoretically by make connections between espoused theory and practice (Gould, 1996).

Service user and carer perspectives

Linked to the discussion about knowledge for and of practice is the association of reflective practice with another high-profile dimension of social work practice – the promotion of empowering professional relationships and articulation of service user and carers voices. Reflective practice has an important contribution to make to these activities.

Working reflectively encourages and is intrinsically bound up with relationship-based approaches to practice (Ruch, 2005). Reflective practice necessitates being attentive to the uniqueness of each human situation. It is not difficult to see how practitioners who have developed their reflective capabilities are more alert to and respectful of the challenges of working with diversity and difference. This enhanced awareness derives from reflective practitioners having an open mind to knowledge informing practice, one source of this knowledge being service user and carer perspectives. In order to develop as holistically reflective practitioners, able to reflect from technical, practical, process and critical perspectives (discussed later in the chapter), necessitates taking on board the experiences and views of service users and carers. By placing greater importance on these perspectives, practitioners are able to engage with and intervene in family situations in ways which recognise and mobilise their strengths and resources and which maximise the intervention outcomes. In addition, a reflective stance is closely aligned with empowering and anti-oppressive perspectives and requires practitioners to be both conceptually and morally aware and informed (Stepney, 2000).

Anxiety, emotions and reflective practice

The anxiety-provoking and emotionally charged nature social work makes it even more important for the knowledges informing practice to embrace the realities of practice. Psychodynamic theories provide a framework for understanding how holistic approaches to social work practice, informed by diverse knowledge sources, are crucial for effective social work practice.

Psychodynamically informed approaches suggest that the emotional impact of social work on practitioners, and in particular the effects of professional anxiety on workers, can be a primary cause of ineffective or negligent professional conduct. In her seminal paper 'Social Systems as Defences against Anxiety', Isabel Menzies-Lyth (1988) details work she undertook within a hospital that focussed on how the behaviours of nurses could be understood as a defence against the anxiety-provoking nature of the work they were undertaking – work with sick and dying people. The tendency to depersonalise the professional encounter – 'the liver in bed nine'– and to resort to elaborate rituals – bed-making and complex procedures for the dispensing of medication – were recognised by Menzies-Lyth as entrenched, professionally acceptable strategies for coping with the anxiety-provoking professional context. More recently, Beckett *et al.*, (2007) have drawn on Menzies-Lyth's ideas in the context of decision-making in child care cases.

It is not difficult to identify similarly defensive behaviours within social work contexts – elaborate referral procedures and decreasing time spent in face-to-face encounters for example. Unfortunately it is all too rare in social work contexts for the anxiety-ridden nature of the work to be given sufficient or serious enough attention. A recent example of such an oversight is the Laming Inquiry into the death of Victoria Climbié (DoH, 2003), that focused, almost exclusively, on the procedural and practical dimensions of the social work task (Cooper, 2005). This is not to deny the importance for sound practice of efficient bureaucratic systems (explored in Chapter 10), but the preoccupation with procedurally correct practice fails to recognise the inherently messy and complex nature of the cases social workers are involved with and the emotionally charged and challenging behaviours and circumstances they face on a daily basis. Hostility, anger, frustration, non-co-operation are common emotional responses exhibited by families with whom social workers engage. The consequences of children experiencing emotional and physical pain, betrayal and abandonment are the 'bread and butter' of social workers' caseloads. Several inquiry reports (Blom-Cooper *et al.*, 1987; DoH, 2003) include references to the occasions when social workers made visits to families and failed to see the child(ren), either because the family were out or because they were satisfied by the adults' accounts of the children's well-being. In a similar vein, how many practitioners would not admit to feelings of relief when on ringing a doorbell to undertake a difficult home visit there is no reply or when a child does not turn up for a planned session?

With such difficult prevailing conditions it is understandable, although not condonable, that practitioners have difficulty 'holding the child in mind' and 'turn a blind eye' (Cooper, 2005) to the unbearable experiences encountered by some children and families. Bowlby (1988) refers to practitioners 'knowing what they don't know', another version of 'turning a blind eye' – not acknowledging what is seen/known. These are complicated and paradoxical professional dynamics but unless attention is paid to the affective and anxiety-generating aspects of the work the scope for effective interventions that promote positive change (a requirement of post-qualification training) will be seriously diminished and the long-standing problems of retention and recruitment in the social work profession will persist.

Reflective Activity

- Think of a child or family on your caseload who has had particular emotional impact on you. Can you describe the feelings this has evoked?
- Can you work out why this is?
- What impact has this had on your responses to the child or family?
- What has helped or could help you understand and manage these emotions?

Developing a reflective stance is an important way of engaging with and managing these difficult, often emotionally unbearable, situations.

What is reflective practice?

Reflective practice has emerged in the recent years in the professional social work arena in response to the failure of orthodox, technical–rational understandings of knowledge to provide an effective framework for practice (Gould, 1996). There is considerable literature in the professional disciplines of nursing, education and social work that explores understandings of reflective practice (Johns, 2004; Ixer, 1999, 2000; Rolfe *et al.*, 2001; Ruch, 2005; Schon, 1983,1987). Within this literature there is a common acceptance that reflective practice is an elusive concept that has proved difficult to define and is understood differently across different professions. The work of Donald Schon (1983, 1987) is widely recognised across the professions as being of seminal importance to understandings of reflective practice. Schon distinguished between technical–rational and practical moral knowledge, in a similar way to the definitions of knowledge sources, and suggested that 'softer' practical moral knowledge was of as much importance in professions, such as social work, as the technical–rational knowledge sources. The quote for which Schon (1983:42) is now renowned refers to how:

> *In the varied topography of professional practice, there is a high, hard ground where practitioners can make use of research-based theory and technique, and there is a swampy lowland where situations are confusing 'messes' incapable of technical solution.*

For Schon reflective practitioners were professionals who recognised and embraced the 'swampy low-land' and 'confusing messes' associated with the uncertainties and complexities of practice and drew on an holistic and diverse range of knowledge to inform their responses. An important distinction identified by Schon, which has gone on to be a cause of much debate (Eraut, 1995), is between reflection-on-action, after the event, and reflection-in-action, during the event. Schon suggests that reflection-in-action is the more skilled position. As practitioners develop their reflective capabilities they are able to reflect whilst engaged with another person and thereby alter the interaction 'on the spot'.

By drawing together the different ideas about what constitutes reflective practice it is possible to identify four broad categories: technical, practical, critical and process reflective practice (Ruch, 2002, 2007). Before briefly outlining the features of each type of reflective practice it is important to underline that they are not mutually exclusive categories and any one practitioner can demonstrate all or some of the different approaches at any one time.

Technical reflective practice

This type of reflective practice is probably the one most practitioners would recognise and claim to practice. It has three key features:

- It involves reflecting after an encounter or intervention – Schon's reflection-on-action.
- It believes straightforward 'technical' responses can be identified and implemented.

- It requires practitioners to reflect on an encounter by asking themselves *what* they did and *how* they did it and what they would do next time and how.

The focus of this type of reflection is very practical and at a surface level.

Practical reflection

In comparison with technical reflection, practical reflection is more inclusive in its understanding of what constitutes knowledge. Practical reflection understands knowledge to be relative, constructed, contextual and inter-subjective. Practical reflection, therefore, allows both the formal theoretical influences on knowledge construction and the informal sources of understanding, such as personal experience, practice wisdom, self-awareness and intuition to be acknowledged and informative of each other.

The distinctive characteristics of this type of reflection are:

- Practitioners reflect in action as well as after it and endeavour to respond to their reflective insights whilst engaged in the encounter
- Practitioners recognise the unqiueness, complexity and unpredictable nature of practice encounters
- Practitioners ask themselves not only 'what did I do and how' but crucially '*why*'?

Practical reflection does not simply seek to change the interaction in the future but seeks to understand why what took place happened. The practitioner, therefore, is required with this type of reflection to go 'beneath the surface' and to question their own (and others) motivations, unchallenged assumptions and behaviours in order to try to respond differently. Attending to the dynamics of the interaction is a crucial source of insight. By analysing professional performance, practical reflection identifies and modifies personal and professional assumptions underpinning practice, enhances professional understanding and seeks alternative responses. In subscribing to this approach professionals demonstrate their openness to new ways of thinking, their eclectic view of knowledge and their wish to encourage reflection, with the 'self' and with others.

Process reflection

This level of reflection takes practical reflection one stage further as it invites practitioners to examine unconscious processes that might influence how they practice. Drawing on psychodynamic understandings of 'knowing' and the unconscious and conscious processes at work in inter-personal encounters it suggests that mirroring and transference dynamics are a key component in social work knowledge construction (Mattinson, 1975). Process reflection is characterised by:

- Reflection-in- and -on-action, but particularly reflection-in-action
- 'Why' questions, which are fundamental component of, process reflection – Why did certain behaviours arise? Why did I respond in the way I did?
- An acknowledgement of the uniqueness and complexity of an individual's behaviours and the dynamics of any encounter

The opportunity to reflect, to think about and feel, as well as act on, the relationship dynamics and associated thoughts and feelings, enables professionals to gain insight into the experiences of those with whom they work and their own responses to situations. In comparison with the three other types of reflection, process reflection emphasises the affective dimensions of the reflection process as much as the cognitive ones.

Critical reflection

Fook (2002:41) encapsulates the nature of critical reflection succinctly:

> Being reflective and being critically reflective share important similarities. Both involve recognition of how, as knowers, we participate in creating and generating the knowledge we use and an appreciation of how knowledge is therefore contingent upon the holistic context in which it is created. A reflective stance points up the many and diverse perspectives which can be taken on knowledge itself, and the shaping of knowledge. The important difference is that critical reflection places emphasis and importance on an understanding of how a reflective stance uncovers power relations and how structures of domination are created and maintained.

Critical reflection is made up of the personal elements of reflection associated with technical, practical and process reflection but in addition it seeks to challenge the prevailing social, political and structural conditions that promote the interests of some and oppress others. Understanding the dynamics of power is integral to a critically reflective stance and involves practitioners examining their own and other peoples' conscious and unconscious motivations, assumptions and prejudices.

How can reflective practice be facilitated?

Having identified why reflective practice is important and what it is, it is necessary to consider how it can be facilitated. Putting it into practice and becoming a reflective practitioner is not an easy process (Harrison and Ruch, 2007). The attention paid above to the existence and implications of anxiety and emotions in social work practice was not intended to discourage or dishearten practitioners. Rather it ensures they engage in their work with realistic expectations of what is required and what they need in terms of support mechanisms to ensure their practice is as reflective, effective and ethical as possible. Two conceptual frameworks which are central to thinking about how reflective practice can be facilitated are emotional intelligence and the learning organisation.

Emotional intelligence

The concept of emotional intelligence first came into the public domain with the work of Daniel Goleman (1996) 'Emotional Intelligence: why it can matter more than IQ'. Emotional intelligence is understood to be the ability 'to motivate oneself and persist in the face of frustrations; to control impulse and delay gratification; to regulate one's moods and keep distress from swamping ability to think; to empathise and to hope.' (Goleman, 1996, cited in Morrison, 2007). In Goleman's model of emotional intelligence there are four key components:

- Self-awareness and self management (known as intra-personal intelligence)
- Awareness of others/empathy and relationship skills (known as inter-personal intelligence)

It is not difficult to see the parallels between emotional intelligence conceptualised in this way and reflective social work practice yet, surprisingly, the connection between emotional intelligence and social work in general, and reflective practice in particular, has been slow to be recognised.

Morrison's recent paper (2007), from which the above definition citation is taken, begins to develop some interesting ideas about how emotional intelligence can be understood to be a fundamental component of competence in social work practice. From this perspective, it is possible to see how recognising and facilitating the role of emotional intelligence in social work, is one way of addressing anxiety and emotion in practice and promoting reflective practice.

Research (Ruch, 2004) into the conditions that facilitate reflective practice and subsequent work on the notion of 'thoughtful' practice (Ruch, 2007a) identified several characteristics that can be attributed to holistically reflective practitioners, i.e. practitioners who engage in reflection beyond the technical level:

- Open-minded in their willingness to explore alternative perspectives and address uncertainty, complexity and risk
- Mindful and whole-hearted in their ability to engage with the content and process of practice encounters
- Responsible and responsive in terms of their commitment to work in partnership with families in relational and empowering ways

Such practitioners, I would argue, have qualities that might be closely aligned with those associated with emotional intelligence – resilience, tolerance, commitment and optimism. On the basis of this information, along with the emotional intelligence literature, it could be argued that having emotional intelligence is an individual and innate characteristic. Such practitioners will find individual reflective tools, such as reflective journals and critical incidence analysis to name two of the ones most common ly used (see Chapter 1 in Wilson *et al.*, 2008), helpful in their development. Within the PQ framework, the practice assessors can play a key role in enabling practitioners to develop their reflective skills. Reflective logs, as illustrated in the excerpt below, encourage the development of reflective skills which can become an integral part of their routine practice:

> I found the family's 'lack of emotion' a real struggle for me personally, as the family presented almost as seeing what happened to their daughter as inevitable, and that they could not have prevented it, even though to me there were clear indicators over the years – I must be aware not to allow my own emotion to inhibit my professional role, or place judgements on the family. I do not feel I did allow my personal feelings/frustrations to get in the way, however, I must always continually be aware of this.
>
> (PQ candidate)

However, what the research cited above highlighted was that all practitioners have the capacity to develop into reflective practitioners and to enhance their emotional intelligence provided the right conditions exist in which they can be nurtured and flourish. Utilising individual reflective tools such as those mentioned is a necessary, but not sufficient, aspect of emotionally intelligent reflective practice. So what might emotionally intelligent and reflective support systems look like and what is needed to facilitate their development?

Reflective and emotionally literate support systems

In answer to the first question – the characteristics of reflective forums – it is clear there need to be spaces where practitioners feel safe and can express the unavoidable feelings of vulnerability and anxiety that the work provokes. Morrison (2007), referring to assessment frameworks in child care social work suggests that the negligible attention paid in these frameworks to emotions may be related to inadequate understandings about feelings. It is not difficult to draw parallels with the shortcomings of support systems in child care social work contexts which are frequently criticised by practitioners for the disproportionate amount of time spent on management-related activities as opposed to the professional support and developmental needs of the practitioner. Feelings appear to be overlooked. In fact it has been notable how many practitioners in their PQ assignments have felt that the programme's emphasis on the emotionally demanding nature of child care social work, reflective practice and practitioner well-being has given them permission to talk about feelings more openly and make demands on their organisation for opportunities to do this on a regular basis.

Three of the most familiar collective forums for professional development are supervision, co-working and group supervision. In recent years with the emergence of a performance culture and managerially driven work places all three types of support have become less prevalent and/or changed in their focus. For these forums to be effective in supporting the development of reflective practice, they must have several core characteristics:

- They must provide safe spaces for practitioners where they can experience dependency and vulnerability, necessary prerequisites of coping with anxiety, uncertainty, emotionally charged work and risk.
- They need to be sustained spaces, i.e. to be provided on a regular basis and not simply as one-off support mechanisms in a crisis situation. It is only through practitioners developing trusting relationships with supervisors and colleagues that the openness, vulnerability and dependency associated with a reflective stance will be able to develop. Modelling reflective forums on the principles of reflective conversations, discussed in Chapter 9, is one possible way of achieving this.
- There should be a range of forums which collectively address the management, support and development needs of practitioners. Up until recently there has been an expectation that individual supervision can address all three domains of professional practice. The remit of individual supervision, however, has altered in response to the demands of the 'performance culture' and become a primarily workload management tool. Of the three functions of supervision – management, education and support – it is the former which has been prioritised and, as previously mentioned, for many practitioners the educative and developmental dimensions are often non-existent. To ensure developmental and support needs are provided for other forums, e.g. case discussion groups, consultation forums with clear remits need to be established (see Harrison and Ruch, 2007; Ruch, 2007b) for more details of what these forums might look like).
- They should encourage shared, transparent communication and supportive opportunities for practitioners to gain insight into particular skills, values and prejudices and, therefore, the potential for more transparent and less defensive practice.

It is crucial that practitioners have a safe space in which they can voice their doubts and uncertainties and explore various ways of approaching challenging pieces of work. As a consequence the scope for doubt and uncertainty to be voiced is increased alongside an increase in the scope for risk taking and creative practice. Without such spaces practitioners are forced onto their own resources and are insufficiently nurtured to sustain working in a reflective manner for very long. The recent problems in recruitment and retention of social workers bear this out. Team managers would do well to recognise the potential benefits of such collaborative and communicative systems and take steps to ensure they exist in the interests of effective service provision, practitioner well-being and staff retention.

What is all too apparent, however, from comments made by practitioners on the PQ programme is that their confidence in such opportunities and forums being available to them is undermined by their experience of the wider organisational context in which they are located and its inability to recognise the professional development needs of it practitioners (Ruch, 2006). This is where the concept of the learning organisation comes into play.

Learning organisations

Learning to manage and respond to emotionally demanding work has to be central to a learning organisation within a social care setting. It is all very well for individual practitioners to be motivated to develop their reflective skills and levels of emotional intelligence but without the backing of their organisation, and for most practitioners this means their frontline manager, the extent to which they can achieve this will be limited. Learning organisations, or what have also been termed 'intelligent organisations' (Statham, 2004:164) need to develop ways of:

> *surfacing information and intelligence that is normally given low status in policy, service and organisational development. It requires not only that individuals learn how to learn but also embedding this within the way that the organisation routinely operates.*

It is particularly important to emphasise the use of the words 'routinely operates' as it is more common for the learning organisation concept to be closely affiliated with serious errors in professional practice and 'near misses'. When affiliated to the 'making of mistakes', which in child care social work means the death of a child, the concept of a learning organisation is too narrowly defined and becomes unhelpfully associated with the blame culture which pervades professional practice. Part of the reason practitioners are reluctant to acknowledge their emotional responses to their work is the fear of being labelled inadequate or unable to cope. Instead what develops is a climate of denial and disassociation.

A more helpful and potentially more effective conceptualisation of the learning organisation would be one based on routine operations, experiences and knowledge. Such an organisation would then be asking: What is the daily experience of social workers like? How do they make sense of their experiences and produce knowledge, understanding and action from the information gathered? Learning from child care tragedies should not be dismissed as unimportant. Refocussing the remit of learning organisations to the daily demands of the job could significantly reduce the likelihood of a tragedy or a 'near miss' occurring in the first place. It could also contribute to greater value being placed on social workers professional expertise, a reconceptualisation of what constitutes a 'near miss' or a 'mistake' (for which there is work in progress under the auspices of SCIE) and has the capacity to reduce the toxic influence of the currently all-too-pervasive blame culture.

One very practical way of expanding the focus and orientation of learning organisations from exceptional errors to routine practices would be to support the development of forums of the type outlined above. In addition making similar forums available to frontline managers, an overlooked but crucial component of effective, reflective learning organisations (Statham, 2004), would be another step in the right direction. To be relevant and effective, managers need to remain in touch with the demands of practice and not allow powerful managerial expectations to detach them from the emotionally charged realities of frontline practice.

Reflective Activity

Think about the sources of support available to you in your organisation.

- Which aspects of these support systems do you find helpful and why?
- What else would you like to see in place?

Conclusion

Anxiety-ridden reactions are rarely accurate or effective, yet they are common occurrences in social work practice. Part of the explanation relates to the risky circumstances in which social workers find themselves. Equally significant is the pressure on social workers to 'get it right' – the societally derived pressure to act neither too quickly or too slowly or to intervene neither too little nor too much (Ruch, 2007a). With fear from within and pressure from without it is no wonder social workers develop avoidant behaviours, 'blind eyes' (Cooper, 2005) to cope with their professional responsibilities. According to Martyn (2000:6):

> the need for intellectual rigour, organisational efficiency and careful planning is heightened by the emotional intensity of the work.

Reflective practice is an important source of support for practitioners working in anxiety-ridden environments. By developing reflective strategies practitioners avoid what Martyn (2000) refers to as a reactive response, i.e. event-reaction-action and instead adopt a reflective stance of event-reflection-action. This is a vital skill to acquire as it ensures that each situation is assessed on its own merit and attention to issues of diversity and difference are to the fore. From such a reflective position practitioners are better equipped to withstand the considerable demands arising in practice and to practice in more effective and ethical ways in the best interests of the people with whom they are engaged.

Chapter summary

- Reflective practice is a contested concept and one that is challenging to understand, develop and sustain
- Reflective practice challenges entrenched and narrow understandings of knowledge
- The inevitability of encountering in practice painful emotions in general and anxiety in particular makes it imperative that practitioners develop their reflective capabilities to ensure they do not 'turn a blind eye' to these challenges and complexities
- Four types of reflective practice can be identified – technical, practical, process and critical
- To realise and sustain their reflective potential practitioners need managers who embrace the importance of emotionally literate practitioners and organisations that are open to learning

Reflective questions

What sort of a reflective practitioner do you consider yourself to be?

Can you identify a piece of work that has benefited from you taking a reflective stance?

What would help you develop your reflective capabilities?

Chapter 4

Observational practices in working with children and families

Gillian Ruch

Chapter learning aims

- To develop understanding of the role of child observation and its contribution to reflective practice
- To encourage familiarity with the requirements of the Tavistock Model of child observation
- To help practitioners' to recognise the challenges of and obstacles to learning and professional development and the distinctive learning and professional development opportunities generated by child observation

Introduction

This chapter builds on the previous one and explores an approach to reflective practice that requires practitioners to engage with the process of observation and the thoughts and feelings it provokes. Observation skills are fundamental to sound practice and in promoting their development several of the core requirements of post-qualification training (GSCC, 2005) are met, including enhancing skills in communicating and undertaking direct work with children and expanding knowledge of child development. Two of the most important characteristics of the process of child observation are its capacity firstly, to embrace holistic understandings of knowledge and secondly, to encourage practitioners to engage in 'thoughtful' practice (Ruch, 2007a) and to resist premature or repetitive 'doing' activities associated with 'thoughtless' practice. The tendency for practitioners to rush into action is explored in the opening section of the chapter in relation to the place of thinking in contemporary social work practice and the obstacles to 'thoughtful' practice. The following section addresses the substantive focus of the chapter – the nature and purpose of child observation, drawing on the observation model first implemented by the Tavistock clinic. In concluding the chapter, the key learning outcomes associated with the observation experience are identified along with broader applications of the observation model.

Thinking and knowing in contemporary practice

Within social work there is a constant requirement for practitioners to juggle the competing demands to think, to feel and to act (Martyn, 2000). In the current climate, driven by performance indicators and bureaucratic requirements (Gupta and Blewett, 2007) the balance appears to be tipped towards activity and 'doing'. Far less time and attention appears to be given to thinking and reflecting, which by implication, I would argue, involves feeling. In a recent article (Ruch, 2007a), I referred to the following encounter, which vividly illustrated this preoccupation with 'doing'. On two quite separate occasions, I met with colleagues working in education (an educational psychologist and a teacher) who commented on their experiences of working with social workers. In both cases they referred to their concern at the social workers inability to stop and think. The educational psychologist offered a very graphic image of a social worker in a planning meeting drumming her fingers on the arm of a chair and behaving in ways that the educational psychologist interpreted as the social worker's need 'to get on and *do* something'. The social worker appeared unable to stop and thoughtfully consider the best plan of action.

This pressure to 'do' something is not an unfamiliar one in social work circles and derives from a mixture of societal and professional expectations (Ruch, 2006). This pressure is exacerbated, however, according to Bower (2003: 143), in child protection cases, which produce:

> *a particular pressure on workers to act rather than to think and this is exacerbated by the persecutory and unsupportive climate of current social work practice. The service delivery climate which now pervades the whole area of public services also produces pressure to do or provide, rather than to think.*

The challenge practitioners face is in managing the 'thinking-feeling-doing' tension in a creative and effective way. The practice approach outlined below endeavours to support practitioners in rising to this challenge, an approach that might stop the social worker referred to earlier needing to 'drum her fingers'.

The nature of the observational experience

Two perspectives dominate the literature on observation: the scientific model drawing on 'objective' measurements of behaviour (Fawcett, 1996) and the narrative model that describes behaviour and adopts a 'subjective' perspective, which addresses the observation process and experience as well as the content of the observation. This chapter focuses on a narrative model of observation most commonly associated with social work education and practice, which is frequently referred to as the

Tavistock Model. The origins of this particular child observation model date back to the 1960s and Esther Bick's seminal work at the Tavistock Clinic where this form of learning was introduced on child psychotherapy training courses. The three key characteristics of this model, which has been widely written about (Bridge, 1999; Bridge and Miles, 1996; Briggs, 1992; King, 2002; Le Riche and Tanner, 1998; McMahon and Farnfield, 1994; Miles, 2004; Ruch, 2007a; Trowell and Miles, 1991; Wilson, 1992) are:

• Observing the same child over an extended time period on a weekly basis for one hour at a consistent time
• Observing without taking notes
• Attending regular seminars in which group members take turns to present and discuss their recordings of observations with their peers

In post-qualification contexts, child observation is usually based on a modified version of the traditional Tavistock Model. Practitioners are required to observe a pre-school age child in a day care setting for between six and ten sessions lasting approximately one hour. Before they embark on the observation experience practitioners attend an introductory session that outlines the principles of the observation process. As a working definition child observation can be understood as an educational approach which:

> teaches a particular way of being, an attitude and approach which enables the worker to be responsive rather than intrusive. This involves learning how to monitor feelings and reactions and how these can inform, rather than distort, what is observed through the senses.
>
> (Ellis et al., 1998:21)

The rationale for child observation is multi-faceted but it has become recognised as a rich source of learning (Trowell and Miles, 1991). Chapter 8 explores the learning outcomes for practitioners in greater detail but the key components are:

• The observer identity – observation contributes towards an enhanced understanding of professional identities and roles and the ability to think and reflect before doing – learning to observe before intervening, a stance which contributes to enhanced emotional literacy and professional maturity.
• Child development – observation affords a more holistic understanding of child development that focuses on 'normal' development and not simply pathological development and embraces emotional development alongside physical, social and cognitive development.
• Personal–professional identities – an awareness of the powerful dynamics involved in relationships and heightened self awareness from personal and professional perspectives.
• Anti-oppressive understanding – observation strips bare embedded assumptions and values and through the 'safe space' of the seminar groups practitioners are able to explore issues of power and prejudice.
• Physical-psycho-social-politico contexts – observation highlights the enmeshed web of factors impacting on a child's experience that stretches from a child's developmental capabilities through to the prevailing policy agenda impacting on day care provision.

In beginning their observations, practitioners are offered a number of guiding principles that should inform their engagement with the observation task:

- As far as possible, retain the role of observer – 'simply observe'.
- Where and whenever possible, avoid initiating or responding to overtures from children or staff.
- Concentrate on factual description.
- Avoid premature interpretation or theorising.

For many practitioners encountering this model and its requirements for the first time is quite a daunting experience. Fundamental to the observation process is an understanding of 'everything' being significant, from the initial negotiations through to the final recording. Consequently, all aspects of the observation experience need to be thought about and the seminars are a crucial forum in which detailed thinking takes place about the experiences practitioners have encountered and how they can be understood. In the following sections, the four key stages of the observation process – identifying a child, doing and recording the observation and participating in the seminar group – are outlined, and the common difficulties and dilemmas faced at each stage are discussed.

Identifying a child to observe

It can be quite daunting for practitioners to identify an institution to approach. This is particularly the case if a practitioner is uncertain or ambivalent about the nature or purpose of the observation process and task. Introductory letters are provided which explain to prospective day care staff what is involved. In many instances, institutions are familiar with the request as observation is a core component of many nursery nurse training programmes.

Once an institution has agreed to a practitioner undertaking their observations with them it is necessary for them to identify a 'normal' child to be observed. Considerable emphasis is placed on the word 'normal' as it is not an expectation of the observation process that practitioners will intentionally undertake a professional assessment or knowingly observe a child about whom there are concerns. That is not to say that such concerns might not arise in the course of the observation process, but as far as possible they are screened out before hand. Prior to commencing their observations, practitioners are encouraged to consider the type of child (e.g. age, gender, ethnicity) they might prefer to observe and why this might be. Understanding personal/professional motivations for choices made and actions taken is an important component of professional practice and one which the observation experience brings to the fore. In some cases individuals are interested in children of the opposite gender to those they are more familiar with. Where practitioners have young children of their own they are advised to consider a child at a different developmental stage to their children. Often practitioners leave the choice of child to the day care staff. This in itself can prove interesting as it is not uncommon for an apparently 'neutral' choice to have other agendas attached to it, associated with the concerns of the staff group. What is crucial is that from the outset of their contact with an institution practitioners are alert to all aspects of their interactions – with staff, children, parents, etc.

It can be very tempting, and part of the professional practice of social work practitioners, to want to find out about the chosen child prior to observing her/him. This is discouraged and not considered necessary to the task. Background information can 'colour' the observation from the outset.

Furthermore, the capacity to remain 'curious', open to 'not knowing' and able to resist reaching premature conclusions are all central characteristics of the observer identity. All too easily practitioners find themselves slipping into the information-gathering/assessment mode that is such a large component of their daily practice.

In gaining access to a child via an institution there is a further level of negotiation in relation to the child's family. How this is managed varies cross institutions. In most cases the negotiation is managed by the staff and it is not necessary for the observer to engage with the child's carers. In some cases this is requested by the carers and in such instances a meeting can be arranged. It is crucial, however, for practitioners talking with staff members or carers to ensure that the purpose of the observation is made clear – i.e. that it is for their own professional development. It is not uncommon for requests to be made to provide a report on what was observed. This is not appropriate and blurs the boundaries of the observation task. Usually if the tasks remit is stated clearly at the beginning it is possible to overcome this difficult obstacle.

The final consideration in the initial stages is whether the observer is introduced/introduces himself or herself to the child. This is a perplexing ethical issue and there is no definitive line taken on it. For some practitioners they consider not to introduce themselves to the child as oppressive and unacceptable. For others, the consent of the child's carers to the observation process is considered sufficient. Once again what is important for practitioners is the discussion it provokes in the seminar groups and the learning that takes place from practitioners hearing the different perspectives voiced and reflecting on their own.

Reflective Activity

Think about what your preferences might be in relation to the child you would choose to observe.

- What would influence your thinking e.g. the child's age, gender, ethnicity?
- Why do you think you have these views, e.g. your own children's age, your own childhood experiences?

Doing the observation

For many practitioners doing the observation is a challenging but rewarding activity. Part of the reason for it being a difficult experience is the unfamiliarity of the observer role. As observers, practitioners are required to position themselves discreetly in the room where the child to be observed is located and to spend an hour watching them interact with other children and staff and engage in play activities. Practitioners are told that note taking is not required. The rationale for this instruction is twofold: first, and most importantly, by spending time writing the quality and quantity of observations is impaired; secondly, by writing, the observer draws attention to themselves and can arouse inappropriate interest from children and, more particularly, unnecessary suspicion amongst the day care staff.

For most practitioners, adopting the role of an observer is a struggle (McMahon and Farnfield, 2004). Some of the more common difficulties (also explored in Chapter 8) that practitioners identify from undertaking the observation task include:

- Being open to the emotional life of children – by closely observing the experiences of a child practitioners open themselves up to the child's emotional life – both its joyful and its painful dimensions. It is the painful emotional experiences which can be difficult to bear (and which in practice, e.g. Victoria Climbié, are all too often avoided). They require practitioners to be open and able to think about them to ensure they do not adopt dangerous, defensive and avoidant responses.
- Being drawn to other children – finding other children than the one being observed more interesting is not uncommon and requires the observer to be focussed and disciplined in keeping to the task in hand and reflective about why this might be the case. Exploring what captures an individual practitioner's attention and what defines a child as 'boring' are significant points for discussion in the seminar groups.
- Feeling bored/falling asleep – struggling with the apparent passivity of the observer role is particularly challenging given the fast-moving nature of many practitioners' work contexts; 'simply observing' is not only unfamiliar but the attention to detail allows the observer to become aware of the emotional dimensions of children's lives; in some instances, this can be disturbing and distressing. 'Shutting down' is an understandable, albeit defensive, response. As one practitioner put it:

The relinquishing of roles for that of the almost innocuous observer presents its own difficulties, particularly for those who, like me, are more at ease in the defined circumstances of a professional encounter. There is a temporary stripping of identity in this process.

(PQ Practitioner)

- Avoiding premature conclusions – without the requirements of their professional role it can be difficult for practitioners to remain in a position of curiosity and 'not knowing', prerequisite of the observation process. Instead, practitioners are encouraged to avoid theorising, intellectualising or interpreting their observations. The challenge is simply to stay with observing.
- Distracted by thoughts/preoccupations from outside, i.e. work demands/pressures – having difficulty keeping to the task when other work-related demands intrude on the observation experience is all too common. Taking the time to consider what intrudes, when and why can help practitioners further understand what can preoccupy them and what they find more difficult to allow space for.
- Resisting engaging with the overtures of children – this is perhaps one of, if not THE, most difficult aspect of the observation process, particularly for practitioners accustomed to engaging with and relating to children. Trusting that children can benefit from feeling 'held in mind' by an observer and not necessarily needing physical or verbal interactions is a steep but important learning curve.

In all these instances, the seminar group can perform an important role in helping the practitioner encountering a difficulty to explore its origins.

The recording process

In making their recording of an observation, practitioners are invited to record in as much detail as they can what they saw. They are discouraged from interpreting the behaviours observed or attempting to theorise them.

Alongside the detailed factual information the practitioner is encouraged to include their reflections on how the observation impacted on them. For one practitioner cited in an earlier article (Ruch, 2007c), the experience evoked strong personal feelings and memories:

> During the observations I often drifted off into my own childhood, comparing my experiences with what she (child) was doing. This was also apparent in my written accounts of sessions, which appeared to reflect my personal feelings regarding her enjoyment of activities I used to enjoy and her boredom in activities I was less interested in. I also found myself comparing her developmental abilities and social skills with my own children, and other children her own age.

The seminar process

The seminar groups form an integral part of the observation experience and are as important a forum for learning and professional development as the observation itself. Each group comprises approximately eight people with a facilitator who has experience of child observation. The groups meet on several occasions and the focus is on practitioners presenting an oral account of their written records of one observation. This becomes the focus of the group's discussion. As with the observation, an important ground rule of the seminar group is that practitioners do not take notes. Desisting from the temptation to make notes, which can be seen as a defensive activity, ensure that the practitioners retain their focus on the emotionally charged material being presented. Inviting the group to focus solely on the presenter's verbal account creates a space in which they can remain more emotionally engaged with the case material. The act of writing defends participants from the anxiety associated with thinking and feeling as it reinforces the tendency to 'do' rather than to 'be'.

A fundamental facet of the seminar group is the equal importance attributed to the content of discussion and the group processes. The model pays particular attention to the professional dynamics and relationships within the group and the parallels with behaviours in practice. The significance of practitioners reading their recordings to the group lies in the capacity of the dynamic delivery of the recording to provide as much information as the factual content of the recording. Attending to the inter-personal dynamics and feelings as well as factual information arising in the course of the discussion, and reflecting and thinking about how they might mirror the observation experience, generates alternative perspectives and avoids familiar reactive, problem-solving responses. Practitioners can learn some essential skills that can be usefully transferred to their practice if they become more attuned to dynamic and process-based aspects of the work they do (see Chapter 8).

It is remarkable how much of the observational experience is conveyed in the manner in which the recording is delivered and received. On one occasion a practitioner delivered her recording to the group in a disinterested and 'depressed' manner, and the group showed little interest in the material presented. When this was commented on, the practitioner realised this reflected how she had experienced the child and the day care context she was observing. The child presented as emotionally flat and the day care context as under-stimulating. Her disinterested presentation style enhanced this practitioner's experiential understanding of how the child she observed might have been feeling. In some instances the brevity of a recording and the speed with which it is delivered can highlight a practitioner's discomfort with the observation experience. In such cases the difficulty they have attending to detail and staying with the process of observing with the apparent passivity that accompanies it is all too apparent. The need to 'do' something, rather than to simply observe can be overwhelming for some people and can interfere with their capacity to 'see' in more detail what is actually happening for the child. The seminar group too can also feel they have not 'got a feel of the child' from the recording they are presented with.

A core characteristic of the seminar group is its role as a 'thinking space'. It is not the place of the group to try to problem-solve or intervene. Rather the group's primary task is to understand better the child's experience. Two theoretical frameworks that help make sense of the dynamics that arise in seminar groups are mirroring and containment.

Mirroring Mirroring is a well-established psychodynamic term, which relates to the ability for unconscious feelings to be replicated in different places In the context of professional practice, it can result in client–practitioner relationships mirroring other significant earlier relationships and also being further reflected within the supervisory relationship (Hughes and Pengelly, 1997; Mattinson, 1975). In the context of child observation, mirroring can happen in a number of ways:

> *The observation process, which requires practitioners to watch and experience events unfold, as opposed to act and intervene in events, involves the practitioner at a conscious and unconscious level … Mirroring processes, in relation to the observation experience, function on several levels. In the observation seminar context the influence of unconscious processes can result in dynamics arising from the practitioner's experience of observing the child (McMahon and Farnfield, 1994) and/or from their own personal /professional circumstances being mirrored in the way the recording is presented, as suggested above.*
>
> (Ruch, 2007c:172-3)

In addition, these dynamics can be further mirrored in the responses of seminar group members to the practitioner presenting their recording. In recordings where the content evokes anxiety in the seminar group because of potential child protection issues, for example, it is not uncommon for the practitioners presenting their recording to feel 'interrogated' by the group and a 'failure'. In the group's effort to deal with the anxiety provoked in them by the observation material, they can resort to a 'problem-solving mentality', which involves asking endless questions in a false search for factual certainty and making numerous practical suggestions about what the observer 'should do'. The group facilitator has a crucial role in helping the group to stay with their affective responses and speculating with the group on the possible origins of the feelings being communicated – do they originate in the child being observed, the observer's personal/professional circumstances or can they be understood in another way? The facilitator seeks to make explicit the mirroring processes at work and to help the practitioners understand their unconscious, affective responses to the observation experience. A central part of the facilitator's responses is to encourage practitioners to desist from avoiding or eliminating their anxiety by 'doing' something and resorting to 'problem-solving' strategies.

In addressing the mirroring dynamics that can characterise seminar group activities, the facilitator, along with the group, is also fulfilling an important role as a container for the anxiety experienced by practitioners in the observation process.

Containment   In an article on child observation and social work training, Briggs (1992) clearly outlines the concept of containment and emphasises the important role of the seminar group (and by implication the group facilitator) in enabling practitioners to feel contained and to develop their capacity to tolerate painful and difficult feelings and what Briggs refers to as 'negative capability' and to avoid 'premature knowing'. The seminar structure which underpins the Tavistock observation model provides an important space in which the practitioners can be enabled to recognise in themselves affective responses that 'mirror' those of the child they are observing. In providing a 'safe space' and 'safe relationships', the seminar group acts as a container for the difficult and often painful or uncomfortable experiences encountered during the course of observation.

The concept of containment, like that of mirroring, emphasises the importance of practitioners engaging with cognitive and affective processes and learning, with each type of 'knowing' enhancing the other. From an anti-oppressive perspective, experiences of containment are significant as they offer opportunities for practitioners to explore issues of diversity and difference in safe contexts. This is particularly noticeable in groups with male practitioners, for whom the observation experience generates sensitive issues about gender and professional identity.

Wider applications of observational learning

Observation techniques can also be applied to different contexts. Organisational observation derives from the child observation model and requires practitioners to observe in an unfamiliar but related professional context (e.g. health care or educational settings) in order to develop more informed understandings of the knowledge, skills and values of different professions and to explore the responses evoked in the observer from their observation of professional practices. This application of observation is particularly pertinent with the imminent move towards integrated children's services and the requirement for closer inter-professional working.

Perhaps one of the most distinctive features of the observation experience is that it has the capacity to engender in practitioners a whole new way of 'being.' A related learning approach that draws on some of the principles of child observation is that of case discussions. Similar to the model of child observation case discussions involve practitioners in suspending their need to 'do' in order to think and reflect on the complexities and challenges of specific cases (Ruch, 2007a). For practitioners who have found undertaking child observations helpful, case discussions can provide an ongoing space where the learning and practice principles they have internalised from their observational experience can be sustained and nurtured.

Conclusion

At the beginning of this chapter it was suggested that child observation is inextricably associated with reflective practice. One practitioner succinctly and eloquently confirmed that an enhanced understanding of reflective practice was a clear outcome of her experience of the observation process:

> However, whereas the notion of reflective practice is widely voiced in social work, I believe that the experience of child observation, with allied reflective seminars, particularly where the sequences are repeated over time, actually goes a step further by internalising the approach in the practitioner. Le Riche and Tanner's subtitle 'Rather like Breathing' (1998) hints at the almost automatic (unconscious) nature of fully integrated reflective practice. This is the most enduring insight that I take from my experiences of child observation, though I am aware it is currently an aspiration, rather than an achievement.
>
> (PQ Practitioner)

If as a consequence of reading this chapter or completing an observation other practitioners can echo these words, then the social work profession has grounds to be confident about the quality of child care practice being undertaken. With practitioners able to think and reflect on the complexities of practice and sustain positions of 'not knowing', the potential for 'respectful uncertainty' and 'healthy scepticism' (DoH, 2003) to develop is increased along with the likelihood of more reflective and effective, as opposed to reactive and avoidant, interventions.

Chapter summary

- Current trends in child care social work make it difficult for practitioners to think and reflect on their practice.
- The Tavistock Model of child observation offers practitioners the opportunity to think and reflect before intervening to develop enhanced practice.
- Child observation requires practitioners to suspend their professional judgments, to adopt an observer role and to experience a position of 'not knowing'.
- Through the process of observation, recording and seminar discussions practitioners have the capacity to develop a heightened understanding of the emotional lives of young children and the wider impact of developmental and socio-political factors on children's experiences.
- Child observation is a versatile and creative pedagogic approach, the principles of which can be applied to other forms of observation, e.g. organisational and inter-professional practice contexts and reflective models of teaching and learning, such as case discussions.

Reflective questions

What is your initial response to the requirements of the Tavistock Model of child observation? Can you work out why this is?

Which of the challenges of the observation process identified in the chapter do you find most daunting?

To what extent do you consider yourself able to hold a position of 'not knowing', 'respectful uncertainty' or 'healthy scepticism?

Chapter 5

Every Child Matters and the context for inter-professional and inter-agency practice

Chris Warren-Adamson

Chapter learning aims

- To outline the current policy context for inter-professional and inter-agency practice
- To reflect on the wider significance of the Every Child Matters agenda and Government priorities
- To introduce complex inter-personal challenges involved in the implementation of Government's endeavours to join agencies and professionals in collaborative practice

Introduction

This chapter introduces several key social policy directions that provide the context of contemporary collaborative practice. In the course of the chapter some policy directions are examined and a number of enduring themes are identified. They include a continued thrust for regulatory, proceduralised and instrumental practice, as well as the encouragement of new, emergent professional groupings, a development which adds new complexity to the renegotiation of roles and territories for child and family practitioners. This chapter complements Chapter 11 which develops a set of ideas about day-to-day collaboration and proposes the collaborative group as a productive way of exploring complex ideas and developing a range of relationships.

The inter-professional policy context

The thrust for joined-up practices is not new. Consider for example the idealism of the Curtis Report (HMSO, 1946) which followed the death of Dennis O'Neill and which set the stage for the Children Act 1948. The idea for the new, post-war Children's Officers in the new Children's Departments was that they should know at first hand the children and young people in their constituency who needed to be taken care of by the local state. At the same time, the very same Children's Officer was deemed to be *inter pares*, among equals, with other chief officers of the local authority. Since then, however, economies of scale, our deeper knowledge of complexity, a profound mistrust of the promise of welfare, have challenged the early idealism.

Since 1997, the social policy and political context of Social Work has been characterised by the implications of New Labour's 'Third Way' (Lewis and Surender, 2004)). Features of the 'Third Way' have included for the first time a child care strategy (Lister, 2006) tied to a policy of education and work for women, and an assumption about children's role in the workforce as social investment (Lister, 2004; Williams, 2004) adding to the tension between protection, need and educational and other opportunities. New Labour's governments have been 'modernising governments' resulting in a plethora of legislation and policy directives, one major implication of which has been the regulation, inspection and proceduralisation of professional practices, not least in social work and education (see Calder and Hackett, 2003; Calder, 2004).

Dean (2004) and Le Grand (2006) have proposed and debated the idea that we are living in a post-emotional welfare state, in which professionals have to content themselves with an instrumental role in the delivery of services and, continuing Thatcher's consumerist society, users or clients of social workers are seen as active, critical and independent. Moreover, one observation is that women are encouraged through a growing day care service to play an even greater part in the workforce whilst men are dealt with ambivalently, encouraged to develop the father role, but also regarded as a dangerous challenge to women, children and families (Kilkey, 2006).

New Labour has continued previous governments' enthusiasm for structural partnerships in the delivery of services (Every Child Matters, DoH, 2004) and specifically the joining of the old local authority responsibilities for children in need and those of education authorities. The Children Act 2004 sets these policy directions in law. Alongside there has been the encouragement of a new cohort of quasi or 'emergent' professionals (Garrett, 2003). These moves bring new challenges to the 'old' professions in negotiating their way with a range of emerging practitioner cultures (Farmacopoulou, 2002; Gardner, 2003). The Brown Government looks likely to sustain and develop these broad directions.

A specific and continuing source of Government's concern for a stronger and more efficient system of regulation and exchange of information about children derives from the well-documented accounts of child deaths and innumerable abusive events which many claim are within professionals' capacity to prevent. Responses over time can be broadly characterised as:

1 Structural – children's departments, Seebohm departments, children's trusts/Every Child Matters, alongside a host of investigatory organisational arrangements
2 Procedural – regulatory and assessment frameworks, protocols for action
3 Technical – predictive measures of a general nature about risk, specific abusive categories, and new technologies

4 Morality and responsibility claims, e.g. *duty* of members, the *child in trust*, the *corporate parent*
5 'More of' measures – training, 'knowledge', numbers, of which PQ training is a part
6 Target-setting and other incentive and managerial measures
7 Supervision and 'look after' measures
8 Practice and organisational theory

All these measures have been introduced in the context of a global, highly mobile changing society, which challenges stability in parenting in families and wider parenting collectives in which, *inter alia*, professionals and quasi-professionals play a part.

Every Child Matters and The Children Act 2004

Two policy manifestos, Every Child Matters (ECM) and its legislative expression in the Children Act 2004, represent the contemporary context for the development of many children's services and set the scene for the contemporary aspirations for a joined-up practice. ECM has identified two key sites for practice – children centres and schools – with the underlining emphasis being placed on education. The priorities of welfare are drawn into these worlds, up to a point. ECM continues to engage with concerns which have endured over the post-war phase:

• Early protective intervention highlighting technology, protocols, managerial capacity, instrumentalism
• The top-down development of practice standards, targeting, performance, outcomes and measurements, and the still poorly understood notion of children's champions
• Skills and recruitment, common core training, inter-professional activity, leadership, occupational standards, assumption of status aspiration

Within Every Child Matters, the Government has identified five main goals for children:

• Being healthy: Enjoying good physical and mental health and a healthy lifestyle
• Staying safe: Being protected from harm and neglect
• Enjoying and achieving: Getting the most out of life and developing the skills for adulthood
• Making a positive contribution: Being involved with the community and society and not engaging in anti-social or offending behaviour
• Economic well-being: Not being prevented by economic disadvantage from achieving their full potential in life

Every Child Matters represents the aspirations for inter-professional working and this is intended to be operationalised through the introduction of a Common Assessment Framework or CAF. The CAF aspires to a continuum of needs and services and seeks to establish a shared early assessment of children's needs that may lead to specialist assessment. The CAF means a single point of contact for information about children, a commitment to share and to take action, and the provision of a lead professional. The lead professional exists for those children who have a number of support needs identified by a CAF assessment and who require an integrated response. Such persons will be a single point of contact for children and can be anyone from the network around the child who is competent to carry out the role. An interesting aspect of the lead professional role is the intention that children and families are invited to identify who they would like appointed as the lead professional. In itself this shift in how roles are defined is significant in the reconfiguring of inter-professional working. No longer will the expectation be that, when there is cause for concern about a child's welfare, it is primarily the social worker's responsibility to address and resolve the issues. This new role of the lead professional represents society's expectation that responsibility for children is sustained and that no one will 'drop the baton' for individual children. Alongside the generation of information between practitioners and agencies, the lead professional is the critical mechanism for improved services.

The above represent considerable attention by Government to improving inter-professional working but these initiatives do not help us as far along the road as we would wish. There is the matter of political consensus about welfare and also that enduring challenge, which is the gap between the intentions of Government expressed through legislation, guidance and so on, and the discretionary, negotiated, sometimes resistant, world of day-to-day practice. In this regard, Halpern's sanguine remarks about similar US intervention endeavours in the early 1990s are remarkably pertinent:

> What are the chances that the current generation of parent support and Education programs will have a more powerful and widespread effect on the early childhood experience of low-income children than earlier generation? The current generation of programs is certainly working from a more adequate knowledge and experiential base than were earlier ones. If that were the principal historical obstacle to greater efficacy for these programs, then a significant technical assistance effort should conceivably put that knowledge and experience in the hands of local programs around the country. But in this author's view, lack of technique and uneven implementation in parent support and education has not been and is not now the most fundamental constraint to greater efficacy. The fundamental constraint is our society's historic, and as yet unresolved, ambivalence about the causes of poverty, communal responsibility for children and families, and the appropriate conditions for intervention into family life … This ambivalence has put the supports we have provided in untenable situations over and over again.
>
> (Halpern, 1988)

From rhetoric to reality

Ambivalence about the role of the state in child welfare notwithstanding, the policy/practice tension is developed in Chapter 11 according to recognition of a number of additional considerations. They include the technical complication of contemporary practice, and also our emerging knowledge of the nature of complexity and complex systems. The latter, complexity, means, for example, that organisations are self-organising and transformative and less controllable than we dare admit. We need, according to David Whyte (Whyte, 2002 – see Chapter 11) to concentrate our attention on trusting more, and developing the creative capacity of the workforce. Specifically this means two considerable challenges (a) how to understand, contain and reverse the distancing process between practitioners and between practitioners and consumers, and (b) how to build safe territory, relationship, and 'stickability'. These matters concern the complexity of human behaviour and its negotiation across systems and territory.

Collaborative practice and human behaviour

Whether in the Laming report, guidance or green paper, assumptions about the workforce tend to overestimate human intentionality and rationality, pay insufficient attention to sites for practice, over-simplify the change process and underestimate our capacity for defensive behaviour. In the following section, some of the obstacles to effective inter-professional working are highlighted and strategies for enhancing its effectiveness are proposed. These ideas are developed further in Chapter 11.

How practitioners learn

Humans do not make rational logical decisions based on information input, instead they pattern match with either their own experience or collective experience expressed as stories. It isn't even a best-fit pattern match but a first-fit pattern match (Klein, 1998). The human brain is also subject to habituation, things that we do frequently create habitual patterns which both enable rapid decision-making, but also entrain behaviour in such a manner that we literally do not see things that fail to match the patterns of our expectations.

(Snowden, 2003)

The implications of Snowden's wise words are that learning needs to take place in nurturing and collective contexts in order to make sense and combine perspectives, and begin to unravel habituated patterns of learning and decision-making. Without such containing contexts (see Chapter 3), effective learning is impeded. The responses of enquiries into child death might have appeared differently had they examined practitioners' process of learning and decision-making.

The nature of change

Family therapists long ago introduced social work to the notion of first- and second-order change (Watzlawick *et al.*, 1974). First-order change is that which is subject to *exhortation*, for example, by Government, written guidance, supervisors in a hurry, desperate marriage partners, and so on. It is regarded to be superficial and unenduring, and essentially ignores the system dynamics which sustain patterns of practice. Enduring change – second-order change – needs system change. Early theorisation focused on homeostasis, the mechanism which pulled systems inexorably back to same states and repeated patterns. Thus scapegoating, for example, was identified as not only problematic but also set the family behavioural pattern. Later theory would probably acknowledge an even more complex process of system *attractors* which determine the pattern of complex groups. The message is, *exhortation – social workers should, must, are required, etc …* – is not guaranteed to work for long. To be sustained and effective, change needs to be promoted by affirmation and encouragement, rather than exhortation and punishment.

Defensive manoeuvres

When individuals or groups feel anxious or threatened, common responses are defensive in nature. Fight or flight mechanisms have long been identified as barriers to co-operative behaviour. For example:

- Denial – don't think about it and it will disappear
- Avoidance – you know it is there but bypass it and/or make excuses in order not to deal with it
- Projection – casting our own feelings onto others
- Reaction formation – a response whereby we take on the behaviours of the person with whom we are in conflict
- Counterphobia – we become aggressive in denying our anxiety
- Displacement – rather than take it out on the person who is causing us grief, take it out on another
- Allied to the above is reflected blame, placed on to another to avoid receiving it yourself
- Rationalising or intellectualising – taking the emotion out of the transaction and concentrate on the factual material, the detail
- Escalation – blowing something out of proportion

Many of the above may be examples of habituated behaviour, often deeply embedded in personal or shared experience. Changing behaviour in the group may need explicit commitment and external help and support. A starting point, and only a starting point, is a strong statement of principle, but note that group process can also reinforce non-collaborative behaviour. Defensive posturing – for example, powerfully uncompromising position statements – and hostile stereotyping – for example, *baddying* other professionals, politicians and national leaders – are common techniques amongst groups, for example, in offices, between nation-states, and between sporting groups. They are especially powerful tactics: for example, they engender a spurious solidarity, they gain others' approval, and they can be a stimulant, exciting, funny, and definitely habit-forming.

In the same way that new knowledge about the brain is changing our understanding of many facets of human behaviour, so too is the specific study of mirror neurons suggesting a new biological dynamic for understanding others and the complex transaction of ideas and behaviours we have come to call culture (Dobbs, 2006). The reinforcement and sharing of cultural practices and behavioural practices – both good and bad – has then an additional biological basis. It adds urgency to greater personal engagement and the active ways we come together to change our cultural practices. We cannot just sit back and read about it.

Sites for practice

In the discourse of social work with children and their families, the assumed primary site for professional social work practice is the bureau or office-based site. It is however perhaps not always the most conducive site for encouraging discretion and breaking the mould of habituated patterns of learning and practice. Other sites – extended school, children centres, family centres, residential homes including foster carers organised collectively – are characterised by quasi-professionalism, informality rather than formality, but nonetheless could be argued to have the potential to provide the supportive and nurturing context for practice.

The defensive practices enumerated above are best challenged and overcome by practitioners based in secure sites of practice, the characteristics of which include:

- Strong mandates to undertake collaborative activity
- Confident managers
- Permeable boundaries
- Collaborative initiatives across settings
- A commitment to continuing collaborative action over time
- A tolerance of the transformatory processes which come from collaborative action
- A diffusion of control

Conclusion

This chapter has sought to introduce the political, policy and administrative context for collaborative practice and its implications, not least ECM, the Common Assessment Framework and the critical role of lead professional. What has been highlighted is the gap between government policy, with its potentially rhetorical qualities and the challenging realities of sustaining inter-professional work on the ground. Whilst government initiatives seek to improve practice by introducing new organisational structures for inter-professional work, what they pay less attention to are the cultural obstacles to work of this kind. In Chapter 11 – Collaborative Practice and its Complexity – these challenges are explored in more detail along with a model that can facilitate in-depth cultural as well as structural shifts in inter-professional practice – collaborative enquiry. It concerns the complexity of human behaviour across territories and systems and aims to develop a personal theory for practice in this domain by examining ways in which the workforce is able to effectively collaborate by developing stable practice and embracing complexity. It involves a set of ideas about the nature of collaboration; lessons from complexity science and our emerging understanding about complex systems; about formality and informality; the components of a culture of care; the relationship between status, practice territory, intervention and theories of change; sites for practice; group and inter-group process; and mindset. It proposes that practitioners are best able to sustain relationships and explore complexity through inter-agency and formal and informal inter-professional collaborative groups.

Chapter summary

- Inter-professional working is central to the Government's welfare agendas and to the new PQ framework.
- The Every Child Matters agenda, programmes and priorities are the framework within which inter-professional working practices are located.
- For effective inter-professional working to become a reality requires both structural and cultural changes.

- To practice effectively in inter-professional contexts, practitioners need a grounded familiarity with the Government's policies and procedures and a commitment to working with complexity, diversity and difference.

Reflective questions

To what extent are you familiar with the details of the ECM agenda?

In your experience of working with children does every child matter?

Given the demands of working in childcare social work contexts what do you feel you need to support you in developing effective inter-professional work and for 'every professional to matter'?

Chapter 6

Practice education and 'enabling others'

Kish Bhatti -Sinclair

Chapter learning aims

- To outline the qualifying and post-qualifying (PQ) requirements in relation to workplace education
- To explore recent policy changes and their impact on the role and task of supervisors, assessors and practice teachers
- To discuss the issues raised by the process of curriculum development

Introduction

Within the recent changes in social work education, there has been a thorough re-examination of the principles, content and process of qualifying and PQ training, framed within a debate about the areas of responsibility of those charged with providing and commissioning educational opportunities. This chapter will evaluate the development of a practice education unit, which is part of the post-qualifying children and families specialist level award programme, within the wider context of practice teaching and learning. Particular attention will be paid to the strengths of the outgoing GSCC Practice Teachers Award (PTA) and how lessons learnt from the past have informed the emerging awards. The concerns raised by those directly involved, such as practice teachers and supervisors, will be examined and related to challenges that have arisen in the curriculum development process.

Practice education in the PQ context

The new PQ awards are part of the reforms on training arising from the modernisation and rationalisation of welfare in the UK, and they replace the PQ in Social Work (PQSW) and the PTA.

The new qualifications offer employers a means by which workforce planning, registration, individual appraisal and continuous professional development can be linked together in a coherent, logical manner. Parity and equal status with related professional groups is a key aspiration and inter-professional components are incorporated in all social work qualifications. The overall steer from national Government is to update provision, extend horizons and meet the needs of the deregulated market place on the global stage, facilitated by the European Union, which is keen to harmonise employment practices and offer employees the possibility of work in other countries under the Bologna Declaration (Dominelli, 2004).

The educational reforms began with the social work qualifying requirements (DoH, 2002:3–4) which state that degree students must gain 200 days experience in two statutory settings with two service user groups based on knowledge of law, theory and core values. Graduates with practice experience are then directed towards the post-qualifying system (GSCC, 2006) which offers five possible pathways (including practice education) through three incremental steps: specialist, higher specialist and advanced. At the specialist level, practice education is a minor component of the mandatory training associated with operational practice (GSCC, 2006) such as work with children and families or vulnerable adults. In general, this is a positive move as introduction to supervision and assessment here offers some standardisation of knowledge and skills to large numbers of social work staff. However, concerns centre on the course content (i.e. the amount and substance), the availability of funding beyond the specialist level and the identity of those who achieve the award. Much of this critique focuses on the specialist level and largely originates from those with knowledge and experience of the outgoing PTA as well as the incoming specialist standards. The fear stems from the central aim and rationale of the larger programme of study, which offers expert, specialist training in relation to a particular service user group. Within this remit the practice education unit appears to be small, basic, 'tacked on' and with a primary focus on operational supervision, mentoring and performance management.

For those wishing to pursue practice education beyond this, however, the higher specialist and advanced awards are available as voluntary pathways and in the long term will result in a small country-wide pool of 'super practice teachers' and 'advanced educators'. In the meantime, employer funding is located at the specialist level and practitioners wishing to proceed further will either be required to prove relevance to operational needs or have it included within continuous professional development plans or find personal time and resources.

The Guidance on the Assessment of Practice in the Workplace (GSCC/TOPSS, 2002) forms the basis for developing practice education curricula, for what is referred to as the *Enabling Others* unit (GSCC, 2007). The specialist level practice educator has been deemed by the General Social Care Council (GSCC) as a *work-based assessor* (GSCC/TOPSS, 2002) with some responsibility for student learning, supported by 'a named, experienced, more senior qualified practice educator' (GSCC, 2007:2). There is an emphasis on the environment within which learning takes place and the notion of the 'teaching team' is introduced. The supervisory training is incremental, i.e. three professional development steps within three domains which are set out as:

• Domain A – organise opportunities for the demonstration of assessed competence
• Domain B – enable learning and professional development
• Domain C – manage the assessment of learners in practice

Within this, the role and task of *Enabling Others* the candidate is seen as:

- Gathering evidence of teaching, learning and assessment
- Supporting and mentoring students and/or staff
- Enabling learning whilst recognising and confirming achievement

This step-by-step approach is echoed within the overall standards for the specialist, higher specialist and advanced awards (GSCC, 2007), which seek to promote basic skills at the first level and critical understanding of methods and theoretical approaches to teaching, learning and assessment at the higher specialist and advanced levels. This allows the individual the potential to move from 'competence in depth' at the specialist level to a 'substantially enhanced level of competence' at the higher specialist level and eventually to take a 'leading role' at the advanced level (GSCC, 2006:3). The standards and guidance suggest that *Enabling Others* fits well within the overall purpose of the specialist award. However, the danger is that most candidates will not pursue practice education beyond this level and may even exit with a limited or distorted view of the subject. In diminishing the practice teaching role here, GSCC may have missed a rare opportunity to hand over the management aspect of teaching, learning and assessment to a large number of staff undertaking employer-funded training.

The activity below is aimed at candidates considering PQ training in general and/or practice education in particular and may provide an opportunity to link existing knowledge and skills to those they wish to develop.

Reflective Activity

Being an *Enabling Others* candidate

Aims and objectives

- Identify current skills, areas of expertise and transferable skills
- Examine interpersonal and communication skills
- Recognise strengths and weaknesses
- Consider areas which may enhance performance

Task – An Individual SWOT Analysis

- Construct a SWOT grid with four quadrants entitled: STRENGTHS, WEAKNESS, OPPORTUNITIES, THREATS. Think about and jot down in the relevant quadrant your personal strengths and weaknesses.
- Relate them to opportunities and threats which may facilitate or hinder your role as an assessor.
- Identify what you may find helpful for professional development.

Recognising and facing the challenges of practice education

Practice teaching and learning has a significant history in the UK. The PTA, although not compulsory, was a professional GSCC award and had a unique status as a substantial contributor to the maintenance of educational standards within both qualifying and post-qualifying social work training (Higham, 2006). Perhaps the biggest change associated with the specialist level requirements is the shift from the well-defined role and title of practice teacher to the less familiar role of the work-based assessor. Student learning in the past has been organised and co-ordinated by a practice teacher, with the designated authority, legitimate power and overarching responsibility to manage, teach and assess students (Brown and Bourne, 1996). The practice teacher has implemented core ethical principles of fairness and equality as well as assessed and recorded the student's development as an ethical, reflective practitioner. S/he has had to interpret degree requirements and put in place structures and systems to meet these in a range of situations. The knowledge and experience brought to the task has, therefore, enabled the student to demonstrate competence at a number of levels. The practice teacher has ensured that student learning is provided in a safe environment which supports natural ability and development, tests a sound and relevant knowledge base, examines attitudes and values, promotes individual understanding and enables the application of research, evidence and data. Procedural as well as conceptual skills have been actively taught and assessed.

Practice teachers have, therefore, contributed a great deal to the content and process of workplace education and although the title has varied, the functions have been well understood within a range of situations and across national/international borders. Whilst local considerations define role and task, the title fieldwork educator is commonly used and understood in many other countries (Doel and Shardlow, 1996: xiv). For example, educators in India and Norway (Boe, 1996; Singh, 1996) use experiential, adult learning and other models of good practice in the same way as British practice teachers.

Traditionally practice teachers have balanced reasonable care and control whilst managing close professional relationships with students (Hugman, 2005). The role and task of those engaged in practice education in the future, therefore, needs to be defined by such experience, in order that supervisors and assessors can capture and utilise communication based on reflective and critical approaches, self-knowledge, use of power and authority. Well-defined structures and systems, which are student-learner-led and values-driven (for example, in relation to confidentiality and privacy) within supervision and assessment are likely to build on best practice.

The development of the specialist level awards has been informed by such thinking within national and local consultation with key stakeholders, including practice teachers and service users, constituted initially by the British Care Councils and by universities. Throughout this process, employers have also retained the focus on case supervision, workload management and workforce planning, based on the future shortage of experienced practice teachers able to support those undertaking *Enabling Others* within continuing structural and administrative change. The consultation has led to some solutions, including the expectation that future higher specialist and advanced award candidates will directly support *Enabling Others* candidates.

The drive to maintain professional equivalence with related professions suggests that PQ is core to the development of social work identity and status, particularly within the emerging multi-professional workforce. As a result the PQ system will increasingly look to a range of professionals to judge and assess the performance of future social workers, as well as promote methods such as group-, peer- and self-directed learning. If this occurs social work teams may need to take greater responsibility for co-ordination and management of learning in the workplace and ensure that students/colleagues continue to benefit from experience based on the one-to-one relationships enjoyed by students and practice teachers in the past. It is clear that the organisational support required by *Enabling Others* candidates includes a willing employer/manager, prepared to invest in the learning organisation and allow the development of a 'teaching team' approach to the quality, quantity and overall standard of work. For many teams, professional development has been a key inspirational goal (Coulshed and Orme, 2006), sustained by the long-term support of practice teachers and training/development officers (Dominelli, 2004).

The development of *Enabling Others* has proved to be challenging for all concerned particularly in relation to:

- Quality and quantity of the curriculum content
- The complexities of competing demands made on candidates being observed assessing others
- The pressures of the workplace
- The requirements of self-directed learning
- The involvement of service users and carers (SCIE, 2004)

In future the candidate's work with students/colleagues will evidence not only their ability but also the worth and value of the *Enabling Others* unit. In the meantime, the lessons learnt from the consultation and implementation process have alerted programme providers to a number of issues likely to be raised by prospective candidates, who may creatively respond to constraints inherent within *Enabling Others*, by choosing one or all of the following options:

- 'Opting out' – in addition to the issue of reduced content, many candidates with relevant knowledge and experience are likely to seek accreditation for prior learning (APL) and therefore miss out on the unit altogether, unless they hold university and professional credits as practice teachers
- 'Fitting in' – candidates on expert pathways such as children and families may see supervision and assessment as a peripheral but necessary hurdle to core training needs
- 'Ticking off' – the specialist award is seen as a consolidating experience and it may be that successful candidates continue to supervise and assess students with no further training input

The needs and requirements of *Enabling Others* candidates require a great deal of further attention but it is clear that personal motivation is key to optimum learning and successful completion.

Developing the practice education curriculum

Practice education is one of three generic compulsory components (the two others are interprofessional working and consolidation of practice) of the specialist children and families pathway.

The *Enabling Others* guidance (GSCC, January 2007) states that candidates taking this unit this should be provided with the following input:

- Introductory methods of understanding, assessing and measuring performance
- Basic principles and approaches to adult learning
- Evaluation of the roles and tasks of a mentor, coach, teacher and assessor
- Consideration of the links between qualifying and post-qualifying programmes of study (including the purpose of codes of practice and occupational standards)
- Core professional values, ethics and human rights
- Preliminary approaches to evaluative and reflective practice
- Quality assurance systems and training strategies

However, in order to translate these aims into a planned programme of study, i.e. the unit curriculum, the foundational nature of *Enabling Others* requires some definition and clarity in relation to the key components of the three domains referred to earlier. For example, whilst the first two domains are clearly based on assessing, tracking and evidencing competence in practice, the third domain (manage the assessment of learners in practice) overlaps with the higher specialist level which seeks evidence-based judgements and quality assurance approaches. In essence, the *Enabling Others* candidate will be taught how to supervise, assess and support a student/colleague through a curriculum which offers an opportunity to enhance knowledge, skills and values at introductory rather than higher or advanced levels.

The *Enabling Others* curriculum should be based on outcomes of learning which, if achieved, should enable the candidate to understand and apply relevant knowledge, skills and values. The overall assessment is likely to be through project work, reflective accounts and observations of supervision with a student or colleague by a skilled and experienced Practice Assessor. Once developed, it is important that the *Enabling Others* curriculum is introduced to candidates in a manner which allows her/him to see it from her/his perspective. For example, the candidate needs to reflect on her/his position in relation to the service user as well as the three other key players: the person being assessed (i.e. the student/colleague), the mentor/support (i.e. practice teacher/educator) and the person who will be formally observing, evidencing and reporting on practice (i.e. the practice assessor). Figure 6.1 illustrates how the candidate may relate to these people for the purposes of *Enabling Others*. The primary relationship is with the student or colleague whose work is overseen by the candidate and it is this person that the candidate will be working with directly through supervision and other methods. The candidate will ensure that the approaches to intervention of the student/colleague meet the quality and standard of service required by the organisation.

Enabling Others is based on principles of adult learning and so candidates are likely to hold a great deal of responsibility for their own personal development as well as gathering evidence of professional competence. There is an expectation that candidates will develop planning, co-ordination and planning skills as well as knowledge of communication, interpersonal and performance standards.

It follows, therefore, that the *Enabling Others* unit includes general ideas and principles of *adult learning*, gathering *evidence of competence* and (based on the understanding of the content of the *Enabling Others* unit) what constitutes a *practice curriculum* for a student or colleague. These three

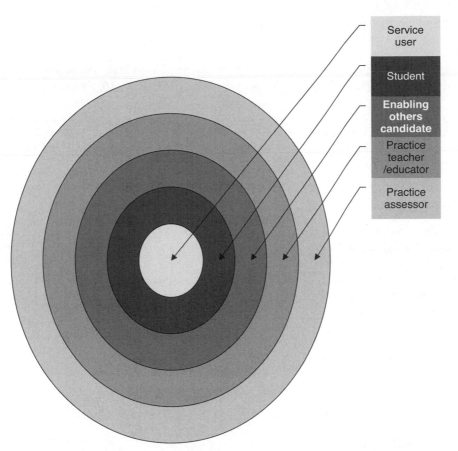

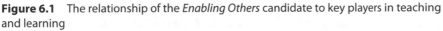

Figure 6.1 The relationship of the *Enabling Others* candidate to key players in teaching and learning

areas offer important foundational knowledge which the candidate is likely to apply directly and immediately in work with the student/colleague. They are, therefore, summarised below.

Principles of adult learning

In general principles of *adult learning*, particularly when used in conjunction with reflective practice, are core to professional development principally because they:

- Improve communication and inter-personal skills
- Increase knowledge of self in relation to others
- Enhance understanding of the team and organisation

- Promote professional growth and development
- Relate theory to everyday processes

Content such as this allows the opportunity for practitioners to make important links between theoretical and applied knowledge in daily practice. Bogo (1996:103–116) refers to this as:

> *The process of moving from concrete to abstract, active to reflective, represents points in a cyclical loop which promotes the integration of theory and practice. …They will be motivated to learn if they perceive that the new knowledge and skill will help them in the performance of important tasks in a current problem solving activity.*

Evidence gathering

For the *Enabling Others* candidate gathering *evidence* is a key task within the process of assessment and requires an understanding of differences in levels of competence as well as the student's natural ability, stage of learning and past experience. At the beginning of the relationship the candidate needs to ensure that individual as well as organisational expectations are shared with the student/colleague. The type and level of evidence also necessitates some discussion, particularly in relation to:

- Validity
- Range and sources (including inter-professional and service users)
- Personal and professional values
- Relevance
- National Occupational Standards

Practice curriculum

A general understanding of the areas above will enable the *Enabling Others* candidate to produce a practice curriculum for the student/colleague, which incorporates the following content:

- Aims, objectives and purpose
- Content of learning
- Strategies for teaching/learning (including sequence and patterns)
- Methods and approaches used to judge performance
- Review and evaluation approaches
- Key documents such as Codes of Practice, Codes of Ethics and organisational codes
- Relevant statements, policies and procedures

The content of the curriculum needs to relate to the organisational context, legal frameworks and geographical setting. The following exercise may offer potential candidates the opportunity to plan, prepare and draft a programme of study as well as consider and collate supporting documents in preparation for undertaking the unit.

Reflective Activity

Developing an *Enabling Others* Curriculum

Aims and objectives:

- To consider the content of a practice based curriculum
- To evaluate the knowledge and skills needed
- To examine how it can be presented

Task

- Individually, or in a small group/team, list the content of a practice curriculum for a first assessed *or* second assessed placement.
- Examine the knowledge and skills you have and will need to develop and deliver the curriculum.
- Consider how you will introduce it to a student when s/he arrives.

Conclusions

This chapter has outlined the historical backdrop to the new *Enabling Others* unit, which is one of the three compulsory and generic components of the PQ framework. In so doing, the concerns relating to the new requirements for practice education have been identified along with core components of the curriculum. It is hoped that the specialist level curriculum will be a positive educational opportunity that allows candidates to opt into it positively rather than tick it off unenthusiastically. Also that it will, in the long term, be part of a sound PQ framework able to meet long held educational standards particularly, given this book's remit, for those following the children and families specialist award.

Professional concerns about the complexities of the specialist, higher specialist and advanced awards and the importance of linking them together have been highlighted. When seen as a whole, the framework appears to have the potential to meet the continuous professional development and registration needs of social work professionals, primarily because it is built upon many years of good practice based on a 'building block' rather than a 'new broom' approach to programme development.

The argument for the maintenance of national standards and good quality learning opportunities originates from practice teachers, gatekeepers to the profession, who see work-based assessors and practice educators as natural successors to this important role. The commitment to the maintenance of high quality education and training is important for all involved, and most particularly for service users, many of whom have given up time, energy and commitment to support the development of post-qualifying programmes of study. Future developments of the new practice education curriculum design and delivery must not lose sight of this good work.

Chapter summary

- Practice teachers and other representatives of social work organisations have always played an important role in the development of policy on practice education. The development of the PQ framework provides a window of opportunity to widen the appeal and involvement of operational staff in teaching and learning in the workplace.
- The further guidance provided by GSCC (2007) confirms the view that expectations at specialist level will focus on the development of basic skills in supervision and assessment and that more complex and critical understanding of methods and theoretical approaches to teaching, learning and assessment are likely to be located at the higher specialist and advanced levels.
- The move from the well-defined role and title of practice teacher to the lesser-known responsibility of the work base assessor is a significant shift for practice education.
- Curriculum development of the specialist unit on practice education must not occur in isolation from the higher and advanced level practice education awards. Often the problems found here may be solved at the Higher Specialist/Advanced levels.
- Three of the central components of the *Enabling Others* unit include developing adult models of learning, understanding the nature of evidence (and how it is best gathered) and identifying the key features of the practice curriculum.

Reflective questions

What is the biggest hurdle for you as an *Enabling Others* candidate?

How can service users and carers be actively and positively involved in the assessment of candidates on specialist awards?

How might you educate your team, colleagues and management to understand the *enabling others* role?

Part Two

The post-qualification curriculum

Chapter 7

Focus on the child

Tim Gully

Chapter learning aims

- To identify internal and external influences that shape the development of a child or young person
- To explore the issues, particularly in relation to risk and resilience that inform our understanding of childhood, children and young people
- To review the impact of government and professionals on the development of the child and young person
- To consider the place of childhood in our times
- To evaluate the impact of natural parenting and state caring on children's development and behaviour

Introduction

PQ Candidate: 'There's no such thing as childhood anymore.'

Me: 'No?'

PQ Candidate: 'They've taken it away.'

Me: 'They have?'

PQ Candidate: 'Government, scientists, the media and experts and that includes us.'

(PQ candidate)

Social workers entering any post-qualifying course of study often speak of feeling burdened by work and exhibit a degree of cynicism about the job they do, about management and about the value of social work itself. They argue that they cannot see the child for the administrative expectation that weighs upon them. In the continuing professional development post-qualification context, any course that is to have a positive impact on candidates has to engage and lift them out of the utilitarian nature of their working life. It is important to pose political questions and challenge candidates to question the current doctrine. To respond to this challenge, this chapter seeks to 'pinge the nerve ends' of the reader in order to stimulate debate and generate critical thinking.

The chapter takes a strong contextual view of the child and assumes readers will already have mapped the rudiments of conventional child development, (Aldgate *et al.*, 2006; Bee, 1997) and perhaps had opportunity to engage with the more challenging ideas of Germain and Bloom (1999) and Saleeby (2001) who mirror in their structure the ideas of tandem development and explore the complex multi-faceted domain of the bio-psycho-social. Drawing on these complex ideas the chapter examines four linked perspectives on child development: the physical, the psychological, the parented and the social child and illustrates the complex nature of contemporary childhood (see Figure 7.1).

The four learning domains

The creation of a child, of a young person and ultimately of an adult is a process in which we are able to identify key areas for learning. These areas touch, overlap and continually influence each other to form a complex pattern of developmental factors. Traditionally they are learnt about separately – biology, psychology, sociology – and to some extent this remains a valid paradigm for learning. It is important, however, that this learning is done within the context of the real world experience of the child and young person, the parent and carer and the social worker. In order to achieve this the different themes that link one domain with the next, elements such as gender, culture and disability and subjective elements such as risk, need to be recognised. The concept of risk, in particular, is a significant factor in all our lives and in our practice as social workers.

Risk and resilience

Risk is an inevitable aspect of life but how risk is defined is subject to enormous variation in time and space. In the Middle Ages, it was regarded as *force majeure* and then gradually it became more generally associated with dangerousness. In the post-modern era, risk is seen as being about managing probability and uncertainty in which a calculation has to be made between factors. For most people risk equals danger, but more than ever it can equate with challenge and excitement. During a recent lecture on the subject, first-year qualifying social work students were invited to record anonymously on paper recent risk-taking behaviours. The list included: driving too fast, 'Cappuccino Sex', gambling, alcohol use and credit card shopping.

It is a paradox that at a time when British society has become prosperous with widening choice and increased freedoms, there is an increased sense of risk (Beck, 1992; Lupton, 1999; Maythen, 2004). Within society, children are seen to be vulnerable to a variety of threats, real and imagined,

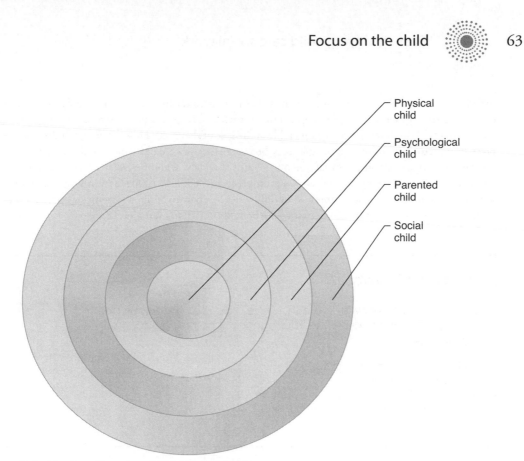

Physical
child

Psychological
child

Parented
child

Social
child

Figure 7.1 The Four Domains of Child Development

from which they need to be protected. People fear sharks and yet it is the coconuts that present the real and present danger[1]. The fact is these 'threats' are comparatively rare and the experiences people have in their day-to-day lives are at odds with the perception created by the media (Thompson, 2002:88). Over-zealous health and safety regulations and the fear of litigation have taken away much simple fun and necessary risk. Playing conkers while wearing goggles, inevitably limits freedom, imagination and play. It is not surprising that parents struggle, as childhood is increasingly a place of conflicting ideas and much uncertainty. Increased calls for children to have a childhood are met by the unreal view that there are now few places where they can safely go. Risks, real and imagined, govern social thinking. In our fears there is a classic tension between the individual and society, solitude and association, care and control, freedom and surveillance. These tensions are about children, yet they actually are entertained within adults and whilst children are over-protected from imagined risks, they are exposed to others.

The reality for professional practice, however, is that risk is inevitable and it has to be assessed, often in terms of factors that are either protective or are seen to present significant hazards to a child's well-being. It is vital to identify the positives as well as the negatives while at the same time making certain the impact of a single difficulty or multiple difficulties is not ignored or underestimated. It is also vital to remember children are individuals. Children are surprisingly resilient but equally remarkable is the capacity for similar issues to impact upon children, even children in the same family, very differently. When compiling assessments it is vital to remember that each child is different and can be diversely affected by the same risk, depending on each child's constitution, circumstances and experiences. These children 'are said to be vulnerable in the face of that risk' (Howe *et al.*, 1999:236). Adversity takes into account all of the factors that may be experienced by a child which could impact negatively on their development and potential outcomes but it is widely recognised that adversity can be experienced at its most damaging when found in multiple forms. Gilligan (2001) reminds us that when dealing with a child faced with a complex set of difficulties it is best to adopt a systems or holistic approach, in other words it is useless mending part of the body if other parts remain untreated.

Reflective Activity

Consider any family with more than one child that you know, one that is not part of your workload or known to your agency; it could be your own.

Ask yourself:

- How are the children different?
- What is the same?
- Are they treated differently in any way?
- What are the points of vulnerability?
- Could they be changed?

The process of scanning child protection referrals illustrates how many will speak for themselves, others will be less obvious and some open for debate. In most cases, however, the hazards will be reasonably clear while the protective factors will be less so. Within practice there is a tendency to highlight the hazards – a conscious or subconscious professional habit or self-protection – yet the positives are as important if not more so. In terms of protective factors Daniel and Wassel (2002:11) suggest that such factors are often associated with 'long-term social and emotional well-being'. It is because of these protective factors some children are more able to cope with adverse experiences than other children.

The role of social work practitioners is to protect children from immediate risk, but also to increase the chances of good developmental outcomes. This can be done by removing risk and/or by reducing vulnerability through an increase in the number or strength of protective factors. Protective factors are described as characteristics or conditions that serve to protect individuals when faced with or exposed to risk. Rutter (2000:658) suggests that protective mechanisms need to be considered as 'a process that modifies a person's response to a risk situation'. Rutter (2000:632) also poses the question: 'Is it more useful to focus on risks that render children vulnerable to psychopathology or on the protective factors that provide for resilience in the face of adversity?' In other words, practitioners should be working to improve protective factors. Garmezy (1985) argues that there are three types of protective factors:

- Psychological such as confidence, intelligence, secure attachments
- Family cohesion such as maternal competence, family size, grandparents
- External support systems such as peer group, school, community, and cultural links

It is these factors that affect a child's experiences and will act against stresses and risk. It is these different, individual resources that help a child react and deal with adversity, but does our care system recognise this, not only in terms of providing positive protective factors, but also in allowing children to take developmental risks?

> *PQ Candidate: 'Children are children and we have to let them take risks. We need to let them have wild times and not impose too many controls.'*

Gilligan (2001) identifies 'variables', 'pathways and turning points' in a child's development. This incorporates the idea that a single positive event or the arrival in that child's life of a single influential human being may change the course of a child's life. Here, it is very important not to underestimate the human impact social workers have and the danger inherent in the current system for moving children between specialist workers. It does appear that agencies have forgotten the power of relationships in child development. Gilligan (2001) argues that this positive factor, albeit a positive relationship that is short in length, could be the turning point for a child's future.

It is well recognised that, despite enquiries, reports, policies and procedures, once a child is within the child care system, the child may drift or have a negative experience. Children are protected or removed from risk only to face an uncertain future. Reflecting society, the childcare system struggles to get the balance right between acceptable, even desirable, developmental risk and unacceptable risk. In the case, for instance, of children with disabilities, are they supported and encouraged enough to reach their potential or are they over-protected, with professionals unwilling to let them experience danger?

Reflective Activity

- Thinking as a practitioner, are the children in your care, on your case load, experiencing enough risk to aid their development and equip them for future life?

Learning points

- Risk is an essential part of growing up for all children
- It is important when considering risk that social workers treat children individually and particularly remember to treat siblings as individuals.
- Remember to consider both risk and protective features

The physical child

The biological development of the child from conception, through the various stages to adolescence was up until relatively recently comparatively straightforward. While there is still much that remains fundamental in understanding growth and development, the debates around health care and healthy lifestyle have become more prominent. Science has taken us from *Dolly* the sheep to the reality of human cloning in little over a decade, genetic modification for choice of gender and appearance is here and the eradication of disability in the womb has surely begun. The physical child, however, is changing. It is possible to think about the physical domain of the child from three perspectives: first biology; secondly, health and thirdly, the appearance of the body.

Biology

In the species sense, it is still possible to refer to the biological child who is like all other children. Each child, however, has a unique genetic endowment. Genes are involved in every aspect of human behaviour; the precise way they are influential depends on complex feedback between the genes and the nurturing that the child is given from conception. This does not mean that the environment overcomes genetics – nurture versus nature – but rather the environment and nurture operate by influencing patterns of gene activity. As it becomes clearer how genes get turned on and off and how sensitive the key segments of DNA called promoters are to a host of influences it is possible to see that the pattern of genetic activity incorporates a record of environmental effects: nature via nurture (Ridley, 2003). Science has taught us that the womb is not the safe place it once was thought to have been, that the foetus is vulnerable to attack for instance from alcohol and drug misuse, from parental stress through the release of cortical and from domestic violence. Advances in knowledge about the brain and particularly neural development are highly relevant to social policy and practice, highlighting the link between a nurturing and appropriately challenging early environment and the apparatus of the brain (Gerhardt, 2004).

Perhaps a more familiar aspect of a child's biological development for social work practitioners is the understanding of a child's physical development associated with the recording of information by healthcare practitioners on centile charts, a common practice and familiar to all social work practitioners involved in child protection work. The average newborn will weigh 3.5 kilograms with a head circumference of approximately 35 cm and so forth. The child's physical growth – height, weight and girth – is time-related and sequential, not so much steady as continuous. Development is measured against milestones such as posture and large motor skills, vision and fine motor skills, hearing and language and social behaviour and play. Infancy is a dramatic period of physical progress, and while a toddler's growth slows, development continues allowing child to jump, climb, run and leap.

There is a danger here, however, that the value of such basic information for all children, regardless of their age and developmental stage, is underestimated. Physical developmental information is essential with babies and infants in relation to failure to thrive or developmental care, but can be as vital with a 10-year-old or a teenager. It appears that the importance of this information is not always acknowledged for older children. It can often be more difficult to gather, is often not so precise, but it is there if we take the time to look. For instance, puberty is a time of rapid skeletal and sexual maturation, but how often is such information included in an assessment?

Reflective Activity

Prepare a milestone chart for a 12-year-old and for a 16-year-old.

• Does ethnicity and /or culture make a difference?

Health

During the last decades of the twentieth century the political importance of the nation's health grew significantly. It had already been recognised that if a nation was to develop a modern economy it needed a healthy workforce and of course the NHS continues to dominate the political scene. The eradication of many serious childhood illnesses and the increase in child mortality have been successes of the system. Recently there has been rapid scientific progress and new technology has brought longevity. Health is now a consumerist environment with self-help, choice and access upon demand.

Child health has generally improved, with a reduction in household accidents, and children are generally safer. Despite these positive developments there are certain areas that remain cause for concern, most markedly in relation to traffic accidents, asthma and obesity. These are very much lifestyle issues. Indeed the health service approach to childhood illness and health has shifted noticeably towards a life-style/education prevention approach with campaigns around sexual health, diet, exercise amongst others.

Through a variety of communication streams, parents are encouraged to bring children up in a healthy way, although what precisely is meant by 'healthy' is a source of considerable debate. Primary school children see food and nutrition, exercise and dental hygiene as key health issues and demonstrate little understanding or empathy for illness as such, unless there is awareness of parental or sibling illness or disability. Pre-teen children tend to see illnesses as having four main types of cause: contagion (microbes and viruses), association with dirt and pollution, overeating and poor diet, being outdoors with inadequate clothing (Bush *et al.*, 1996). Under-sevens see causes as being magical, bad luck, punishment, 'my fault', while 7–11-year-olds have mechanical understanding: 'It's germs' and in teen years there is an increasing understanding of the link between body, environment and mind (Hill and Tisdall, 1997:138–159).

Reflective Activity

• Considering the children and families you work with? What are the general health issues and how do parents and children respond to them?
• Do we do enough as practitioners to include health issues in our work and assessments?

Appearance and the body

How people look physically, how they dress and what they do with their bodies has become a significant and controversial subject in our society. Whether this preoccupation is 'new' is debatable. In medieval society children were regarded as adults when able to wear armour, so is it any surprise the twenty-first century society struggles with child identity and the nature of childhood? Foucault (1978:) refers to 'biopower', the practice of modern institutions to regulate their subjects through 'an explosion of numerous and diverse techniques for achieving the subjugations of bodies and the control of populations'. Writers, such as Shilling (2003), have developed this theme, highlighting the importance of the body as a site for social expectation and individual expression. Scientific and medical techniques, sexuality, celebrity and design have all contributed to the body image debate. Children have cosmetic surgery, spend millions on clothes, fight obesity or not, slim and tan and so forth reflecting the behaviour of adult obsession. Parents worry about the lurking paedophile and yet will dress their children as young adults. As social workers helping families and carers construct appropriate boundaries for children, these social pressures are a source of constant challenge.

Learning points

- It is important when assessing for significant harm that social workers pay close attention to the physical development of a child/young person and liaise closely with health care professionals.
- Practitioners need to be sensitive to cultural diversity and multiple perspectives on health.
- The body is a significant reflector of culture and self-identity, but can also represent the manipulative power of the media, commercialism and the state.

The psychological child

At the end of the nineteenth century psychology brought new explorations of the capacities, desires, needs and vulnerabilities of children, and had considerable impact on parenting and teaching. According to James *et al.* (1998:17):

> Psychology …, firmly colonized childhood in a pact with medicine, education and government agencies.

This period saw the development of Freud's ideas about the 'unconscious child', the growth of interest in the psyche and the emergence of Piaget's model of the 'naturally developing child'. Freud introduced the psychoanalytic method for treating mental disturbance, or controlling some behaviour that was deemed as abnormal or a threat to society. He was the first medically trained neurologist to decide to use purely psychological means to treat his patients. Despite Freud's influence, the use of psychiatry remains a significant method of dealing with difficult children as we have seen during the later part of the twentieth century with diagnostic labelling of children, often with the spurious use of diagnoses such as ADHD – attention deficit and hyperactivity disorder – and the use of drugs such as Ritalin.

Reflective Activity

- ThesymptomsattachedtoADHDcanbesortedwithagoodbreakfastandclearboundaries.
- Discuss.

Piaget's theory places its emphasis on discontinuities in child development, arguing that children pass through given stages of development. He clearly distinguished between development and learning, believing the former to be a spontaneous, structured whole, in contrast to the provoked, limited nature of the latter. His theory is essentially constructivist, avoiding discussions about nature and nurture by considering how the child actively constructs his understanding of the world. One of the main themes is that of adaptation: individuals, like biological species, develop as a result of continuous adaptation to the environment.

Piaget is rightly criticised on a number of points: his timetable of development is too prescriptive, the model is based in Western thinking, and he believed that young children were fundamentally egocentric and, therefore, unable to adapt successfully to viewpoints other than their own. A major weakness with Piaget's theory was his unwillingness to fully consider the degree of interplay between different aspects of development: social and cognitive, social and linguistic, and of course language and thought. Such theoretical points of divergence represent the starting point for a comparison between Piaget and his contemporary Vygotsky.

Although Vygotsky was born in the same year as Piaget (1896), Vygotsky's work and psychological questions, especially about how pupils learnt, did not appear in the West until the 1960s. From then Vygotsky's ideas had a great influence on Western psychology's views of child development, which had up until that point tended to emphasise the importance of the child's own personal cognitive development and the model of the child as a 'lone scientist', as proposed by Piaget. Vygotsky's work attempted to place a Marxist interpretation on the then current theories of child development, language and communication. He argued that human cognition has its ultimate basis in social interactions which are themselves predictably influenced by social history (van der Veer and Valsiner, 1994). The dissemination of Vygotsky's ideas created a tension between Piaget's view that childhood is the road to travel to become an adult and the view that childhood is a time to experience in its own right as advocated by Vygotsky. It is interesting to consider how different our childcare systems

Reflective Activity

- Undertake some brief research into the views of Piaget and Vygotsky and construct a debate regarding the 'Piaget versus Vygotsky question', taking examples from practice to enrich your learning.

might have been in Western society had the teachings of Vygotsky rather than Piaget been more widely adopted.

While the theories of Piaget and Vygotsky remain influential within social work practice, it is perhaps the theory of attachment that has become the cornerstone to our current thinking on child development. Bowlby is of course most famously associated with this theory (Holmes 1993), but others before and after have clearly influenced its development. Like all good theories it is based on common sense. If a child is found to have secure attachments to at least one caring person this will provide support for healthy development and learning. A child who has experienced a supportive, sensitive, loving relationship, in turn gains good self-esteem, self-efficacy and expectations about future interactions. It is such factors that are recognised as characteristics of a resilient child (Rutter, 2000; Werner, 2000). Alternatively, insecure attachments including unavailable, unresponsive and rejecting care givers may lead to a low sense of self-esteem, characteristics evident in low resilience (Lambert, 2001). Therefore, Fonagy *et al.* (1994: 235) conclude that 'resilient children are securely attached children'. Gilligan argues that resilience is made up from 'a set of qualities that helps a person to withstand many of the negative effects of adversity' (Gilligan, 2001: 5).

Resilience is not just about the inner qualities. It also takes into account the way an individual perceives a situation and appraises, approaches and tackles the stress they are faced with. It would appear, therefore, for positive resilience to exist, a person will have experienced a situation that placed them at risk and enabled appropriate coping mechanisms to develop. Resilience is therefore developed through the experience of risk and not necessarily through protection from it. There is no doubt that while increased attention has been paid to the identification and removal of potential risk factors as a means of improving some aspects of children's lives, it can also be argued that over-protection may result in the removal of opportunities for children to grow, develop and adapt in other areas.

Children need to be able to understand consequences, to appreciate boundaries and to take responsibility. A significant part of child development is the gaining of an understanding of right and wrong and developing a moral compass. Initially children will follow parental views, mimicking that said by one parent or another. School teachers will gain an influence, often to the chagrin of parents. As the child grows peer groups increasingly hold sway, as to a lesser extent will the media. Most children will share a reasonably common set of values that they follow through their life, values that will be determined by parenting, peer group contact and so forth. Most young people are reasonably law-abiding individuals and the fear of young people is normally totally out of proportion with the reality, but what of those children who commit crime? There is strong evidence to support the view that poverty linked with a lack of opportunity amongst other factors will influence offending, but that also most offending is committed by a small number of offenders (Cree, 2004). Whilst there has been an increase in knife and violent offences, the number of children committing very serious crime such as rape and murder remains negligible, but when it does happen it clearly suggests there has been a breakdown in that child or young person's psychopathology. Blake Morrison's (1997) book *What If?* about the murder of James Bulger by Thompson and Venables, concentrates on the human tragedy of the events surrounding James Bulger's death and the subsequent trial and makes for informative and thought-provoking reading.

Reflective Activity

Taking the murder of children by children, find out about the circumstances surrounding the crimes committed by Mary Bell, Robert Thompson and Jon Venables.

- Were these children criminally responsible?
- Did they understand what they were doing and the concepts of right and wrong?

Develop your thinking by looking at the Juvenile Justice system in Europe where the idea of criminal responsibility can be very different. In England children are deemed to be criminally responsible at the age of 10, whilst in Denmark it is 15.

Learning points

- Our understanding of child psychology has developed from many sources. It is important, however, to remember that much of our learning is based on white, Western, masculine teaching.
- Childhood is lived as much in the mind as it is in the physical environment and this needs to be encouraged and protected.
- The influence of one individual on a child's psychological development should never be underestimated.

The parented child

In social work, we engage with '… families where that aversion to interfering has been set aside in the interests of the welfare of the children, where private family difficulties have become a matter for public concern' (Fisher *et al.*, 1986:1). Social work practitioners are required to enter homes where they are not welcome, to look in cupboards, check bedrooms and make professionals judgments. These judgments irreversibly change lives. Whilst professionals act with the best of intentions, in terms of natural justice is social work intervention fair to children, young people and families?

There are of course checks and balances – swings and roundabouts perhaps – and there has been significant progress in developing common assessment strategies. Following the *discovery* of child abuse during the 1960s and 1970s and fuelled by a moral panic amongst some professionals, during the 1980s and 1990s society became obsessed with child protection that 'also meant that insufficient attention was given to the needs of parents which in turn can influence their parenting capacity and outcomes for children' (Horwath, 2001: 27). To address this issue, a tool was introduced, *The Framework for the Assessment of Children in Need and Their Families* (DoH, 2000), that encouraged a holistic examination of the children and their families. Using the Framework for Assessment, practitioners are expected to examine three inter-related systems or domains: the developmental needs of children; the capacities of parents or caregivers to respond appropriately to those needs; the impact of wider family and environmental factors on parenting capacity and children and not just the risk to the children. While protection, safeguarding and promotion of the child's welfare remains at the centre of the assessment the role of the parents and wider network is clearly stated.

Of course the structure of families has changed. Until the late 1950s and early 1960s, the norms of parenting and being a child had remained relatively stable since the turn of the century. For adults there was considerable uniformity in terms of when people married, whom they married, the work they did, when they had children and how they raised them. Social and economic boundaries were in place and, in general, adhered to. For the child there were many markers and rites of passage that defined the journey from birth to infancy, to adolescence and into adulthood. These stages are no longer the same as the ones their grandparents and maybe their parents went through such as baptism, school, military service, college, stable employment, marriage and parenthood. Adults and children alike understood where they stood and where they were going. Also the power within the parent/child relationship was more imbalanced as parents told children what to do and they generally did it. The child had few rights and families were in general left to get on with life as long as they adhered to basic principles. A far more eclectic take on parenting, however, has emerged. The traditional 'mum and dad' model of parenting has faded with the increase in other configurations as society and culture has changed.

The statutory childcare sector has also changed in response to our apparently more tolerant society, responding also to changes within the law and expectations from government. This has, however, created something of a political minefield. 'Babies "removed to meet targets"'. This BBC headline (Friday, 26 January 2007) reflected political concern that local authorities were removing babies not to protect them from harm, but to keep up with government adoption targets, the alleged logic being that it is easier to get a baby adopted than an older child. This claim was of course denied, but it does raise some interesting questions in relation to policies on adoption. In 2000, government ministers set a target of a 50% increase in the number of children in local authority care being adopted by March 2006. The idea being that too many children, especially older demanding children, were drifting in the system. This reflects the classic social work dilemma, to act or not to act and be damned whichever you do.

Removing any child from its birth parents is often an act of faith as much as anything else. However well thought through, achieving a planned child-focused approach remains problematic. In reality things happen quickly – a 'matched' foster carer is not always available, taxis have to be arranged to take the child to and from school, luggage and pets need to be catered for. Care in general is not regarded as a good option and it has long been argued that children should remain with birth parents or family, only being removed when significant harm is inevitable. The alternative state system itself struggles to offer 'good enough parenting' often leaving children adrift without hope of a happy family experience. Permanency should only be used as the final option, but foster/respite care can be used successfully when protecting children, supporting families and undertaking preventative work. To do this successfully there needs to be a clear understanding as to what parenting is, as Korbin (1997, cited in Horwath, 2001:256) outlines:

> … the most important reason to articulate what we mean by parenting is so that we have a sound empirical base upon which to enter into a working relationship with families in order to improve a child's welfare.

The aim of human parents is to rear their young to be autonomous individuals who will be capable of participating fully in the culture in which they live. There is a remarkable similarity in this fundamental objective but at the same time there is significant cultural relativity with respect to what is considered necessary for parents to do in different communities and also what is considered to be abuse or neglect.

Korbin's idea of the 'autonomous child' is helpful and links with the idea of looking at outcomes when planning for a child's future. It also raises some challenging questions around local authority care. Are children who are looked after prepared for autonomy? In some cases yes, but in others very definitely not. As with birth parents local authority parenting exists on a wide quality spectrum and comes in many styles.

Bee (1994) gives us these parenting styles:

- Authoritarian (high demand/control; low warmth)
- Permissive (low demand/high warmth)
- Authoritative (high demand/high warmth)
- Neglecting (low demand/low warmth).

Reflective Activity

- In the light of Bee's styles consider parenting you observe in practice and in your wider life. Also reflect on foster care and residential care provided by the Local Authority.

The quality of parenting can be influenced by so many individual or complex combinations of issues from poverty and problem drinking to illness and domestic violence. Quite rightly we have moved away from the idea that the problem is the issue to examining how the problem impacts upon the parenting. For instance, problem drinking patterns might be divided as follows: Constant opportunistic drinking, nightly drinking, weekly heavy drinking and binge drinking (Laybourn *et al.*, 2002) and the questions that have to be asked are: Is the problem of a mild nature or short duration, how is it managed by the parent(s), how is it influenced by the age, gender, vulnerability of the child and above all, can the parent(s) change?

The experiences of parents must be understood and respected and involves balancing their rights as individuals and as parents against those of their children. The environment in which the family live and in which the child will grow up must be taken into account. Does the child have the resilience to grow into an autonomous individual with these parents? It brings us back to the question asked by (Rutter, 2000:632): 'Is it more useful to focus on risks that render children vulnerable to psychopathology or on the protective factors that provide for resilience in the face of adversity?' It brings us to that essential question – prevention or removal? Is it better to eliminate the problem or to provide individuals with the skills to cope with the problems? Or is the more pertinent question: In this environment, for this child, is the risk really significant, or is it necessary for this child to survive and become autonomous in their world?

Learning points

- While there are assessment domains and criteria against which to measure parenting, parents need to be seen as individuals in the same way that children are.
- The term 'good enough parenting' continues to be used in practice – it needs to be used with care.
- The child needs to have the appropriate coping mechanisms to grow successfully in the environment in which it will live.

The Social Child

Reflective Activity

A useful exercise is to buy and read as many of that day's newspapers as you are able, watch the news and scroll through the internet newsroom, looking for stories on children, young people and childhood.

- What can we learn from the media about the young in our society?
- What can we learn about the media?
- How often is the child or young person's voice included?

Whilst each child will have different experiences in the particular circumstances of his or her upbringing it is widely acknowledged that children have similar thoughts, feelings, desires and needs whatever their cultural background and in this sense it is possible to speak of the social child. A useful construct for understanding this phenomenon is childhood, a comparatively modern concept that has been shaped significantly by religious, philosophical and welfare rights debates. Most recently, this argument has been inverted to suggest that 'post-modernity' sets the scene for the 'disappearance' of childhood, as many of the boundaries around children fall victim to the general erosion in definitions and moral attitudes. Society has changed to allow the family and the child to become more important, and while science, government and the media have increased their influence the tension between care and control in relation to children remains the ever present and most important dynamic that individuals and society struggle to resolve. At a time when society is so focused on issues of childhood – including new definitions of the family – it is important to remember that 'childhood' and the 'family' have not always been as they are now.

Aries (1962) claimed to have located the development of the concept of childhood within Europe in the sixteenth and seventeenth centuries. He argued that the development of the concept began within the more affluent middle classes of the time, the majority of children being condemned to historical invisibility, literally in that much of his evidence is drawn from contemporary artwork. He sees only little adults in paintings. Aries suggests that artists could not depict young people as children because there were no children and this is precisely what the artists saw. In the Medieval world, a young person of seven was already an adult. Aries points out that most young people were apprenticed and entered fully into the adult society at an early age. He argues that childhood is a later historical creation that grew into existence in the upper classes in the sixteenth and seventeenth centuries, solidified itself somewhat more fully in the eighteenth century upper classes, and finally mushroomed on the scene of the twentieth century in both the upper and lower classes. According to Aries, childhood did not really penetrate the great masses of the lower and lower-middle classes until the very late nineteenth and early twentieth centuries. Medievalists, such as Orme (2003), however, have rejected the notion that childhood did not exist prior to the fifteenth century, or that the quality of parenting was often poor. Both scholars have presented loving parents, caring teachers and a considerate judiciary that balances the dark view held by Aries and others.

In response to the child's growing visibility, the child became the subject of a philosophical debate. Indeed the roots of many contemporary attitudes surrounding children can be found in Georgian Britain, as society reorganised itself in ways that have come to be defined as modern with the advent of industrial economies, placing increasing emphasis on domestic life and the cult of individuality. Nowhere is this change more evident than in family relationships, as the family came to be based more often on bonds of affection rather than economics. The child, once at the periphery, began its progression towards the centre of family and social life. The Georgian elite discussed the basic nature of children with great intensity and developed the view of the child as a creature of innate evil. This idea had emerged in the sixteenth century, originating in the teachings of John Calvin. Calvinism saw the essential innocence of the child more in terms of a risk of corruption to their mortal soul, a risk which, due to their innocence, they would be less able to resist and which would put them at great spiritual peril. The child, unless trained and disciplined was at risk of being condemned to a life of sin. From this perspective, child's potential for wrongdoing threatens not only the child itself, but also the adult collective and, therefore, demands control.

Childhood, therefore, was a period of training, a time when the potentially wild child could be disciplined into the compliant citizen. Foucault (1998:136) remarks that:

> The classical age discovered the body as an object and target of power. It is easy enough to find signs of the attention then paid to the body – to the body that is manipulated, shaped, trained, which obeys, responds, becomes skilful and increases its forces.

As an example, the eighteenth century Methodist movement saw childhood as a period of innate depravity that, unless driven from the child by discipline, control and absolute obedience, would condemn the child to a life of sin. It is worth noting that the experience of the vast majority of children differed greatly from that of the social elite, a period of training (education) and taming being unavailable to them due to the requirement that they work in order to increase the family income. This lack of education amongst the poor furthered the view of the depravity of poverty as seen from the perspective of the social elite.

Whilst it was still fundamentally about creating the productive citizen, eighteenth century philosophers increasingly saw the child as an innocent creature, until corrupted by society. In *Émile*, Rousseau (1993) took his lead from John Locke, who allied the child with the natural world. He was able to pull together strands into a coherent and comprehensive system – and by using the medium of the novel was able to dramatise his ideas and reach a wide audience. He stressed wholeness and harmony, and a concern for the person of the learner in the education system. Central to this was the idea that it was possible to preserve the essence of the child within the educational system. Rousseau argued that the momentum for learning was provided by the growth of the person (nature) – and that what the educator needed to do was to facilitate opportunities for learning, a theme later developed by Vygotsky.

While Rousseau and Vygotsky were free to discuss the child's mind, most children lived in poverty and suffered levels of hardship. The poverty issue grew in significance through the actions of thinkers, writers and campaigners during the nineteenth century as illustrated in the fictional writing of Dickens and poverty, compulsory education and the treatment of children in the work place became issues for politicians. While campaigns were driven by philanthropy, economic and social control issues also influenced legislation. The idea that poverty causes neglect and was the primary cause of child maltreatment remained with us well into the twentieth century. What has also been central to discussion on the child and child abuse is the responsibility or profligacy of parents towards their children, issues that resonate with today's sociological, political and criminological discussions. How can a balance between care and control be achieved? Is it a case of a creature that needs taming, or one that has been corrupted by society, or something in between?

As the twentieth century lengthened, more and more attention was focused on the rights of the child, the child's voice, child-centeredness, and social competence, and there has been considerable cultural and legal advance in the direction of children's emancipation. The child has risen until its current degree of emancipation is not only perceived by some as a threat to the adult world, but also to children and childhood itself. Calvin, Locke, Foucault have explored how understanding of 'the child' has been so as not to threaten the adult world and to meet their role as a productive citizen. The scientific views of Freud and Piaget appear to have been as much about social control as anything else, about bringing and containing behaviour within acceptable limits.

Having outlined the development of Western thinking in relation to childhood and the place of children and adults it is essential to also consider how non-white, non-European cultures have understood the historical social development of children – the history may be different, but are the issues not the same whatever the culture of origin for our social child?

Although different cultures value diverse social behaviours, there is nevertheless some broad consensus in most societies about what is desirable and what is not. Consensus theory tells us that stability and social order are vital for the survival of society and when in place and operating effectively, social order is achieved. Conflict theorists, however, argue that the key is conflict rather than harmony, that stability is an illusion and social control is the source of unrest within society. Power is considered to be the ability to control others – parents over children – and the theory focuses on the unequal distribution of that power. Deviance might be seen as a positive, inspiring creativity and creating social change. In this respect our attempts to control children and young people's extremes of behaviour may not only be impossible, but counter-productive. Attempting to impose a model of social competence, without properly addressing social responsibility, has not been entirely successful.

Learning points

- Children and young people are not adults.
- Childhood, whilst a contested concept, needs to be protected.

- Society appears to fear children and young people but simultaneously some children are being oppressed and rendered voiceless. It is vital that their voice is listened to.

Conclusion

It is interesting to compare the way society views children today with how it viewed it a hundred or more years ago. Similar themes emerge despite the passage of time. The same fears and expectations are there. A Georgian family would sympathise with today's concerns about 'hoodies', young people's music and spending power and a Victorian middle-class family would have welcomed a government that punished parents for child behaviour. Yet children are now the objects of unprecedented concern as anxiety whether contemporary families can provide a sufficiently stable setting for children's healthy development is matched by fear of the risks the child may be at in the wider community. A 'Child Industry' has developed that continues to grow in many directions, feeding the coffers of business, keeping many in work and providing a source for endless debate. Each new tragedy, each panic brings with it another enquiry, revisions to systems and more advice. While its effectiveness can be debated, there is no doubt it has changed the child's position in our society.

Of course the quote by the PQ candidate that opened this chapter was harking back to an age that probably never existed when childhood was a protected space (sic), a time of long summers, innocent television, healthy food and sexual ignorance. Upon reflection our own memories are often distorted and yet there is no doubt that the post-modern child, in particular during the last 20 or so years, has become the focus for study, protection and training as never before. As another PQ candidate put it:

I found it especially useful to reflect on my own childhood and compare it not only with those of the children and young people I now work with, but with all children and young people. How things have changed!

With one capitalist voice children are given more rights, money and freedoms and with the other demand they are protected and controlled. Hardly surprising that it is not only parents who are confused. In today's society, if there is a time when children are free of responsibilities and the burdens of adult life, then it is short-lived. With the onset of an early adolescence and expectations to achieve, children's lives have become more complicated, more regulated and less free than ever before.

At times as practitioners we forget the links or just make them subconsciously and it was really pertinent/relevant to be reminded of the importance of child development. For example in my reflection I said when I was told that part of the process of child development would involve pre-school child observations I struggled to work out the relevance to my practice with adolescents and what could I learn from it? However on reflection I realised that there were obvious links in terms of early development, attachment and the long term effects on later behaviour of adolescents in my work. It also helped to draw out links to theory with my practice and considered how my own experience, gender and feelings affected the process.

(PQ Candidate)

Chapter summary

- Working with children, young people, their families and carers is a complex and challenging area of practice that requires practitioners to take into account all the developmental domains, but also to place the child or young person in its own environmental and cultural context.
- The factors, from science to social policy, impacting upon child and young people appear to be increasing and it is important not to forget to focus on the individual child.
- Parents and carers need to have their own parenting style recognised and valued if it does not cause the child significant harm.
- Children and young people should have the space to take risks and rebel and not be unreasonably smothered by government or professional intervention.

Reflective questions

Does the construct of childhood have value for the work you do?

Should the legal age for sexual consent be abandoned and a child-by-child approach be adopted?

Where is the balance between government intervention and individuality?

Is the science of child creation out of control?

Note

1. While there is a general fear of sharks worldwide, sharks attack and kill very few human beings while coconuts kill an average of one hundred people per year.

Chapter 8

Child observation and professional practice

Fiona McKinnon

Chapter learning aims

- To explore the impact of the experience of undertaking child observation and participating in seminar discussions from the PQ Child Care candidate perspective.
- To identify practitioner perspectives, views and learning from undertaking child observation training and explore their application to reflective child care practice.
- To offer an understanding of the challenges and implications for social work organisations of using child observation as part of reflective and ethical professional social work practice.

Introduction

This chapter develops the ideas introduced in Chapter 4 which outlined the principles of the Tavistock Model of child observation and focuses specifically on the impact of child observation on PQ Child Care candidates[1]. It identifies the importance of the contribution of child observation to child-focused, thoughtful, analytical, ethical and reflective professional practice and explores the stages of the reflective journey undertaken by candidates as they embark upon, and become immersed in, experiencing the learning. The central theme of the chapter addresses how candidates examine the process, as part of their practice assessment and integrate the learning to promote anti-oppressive and ethically sound practice. Within the body of this chapter, the discussion expands upon how the learning enabled practitioners to refocus on the child, the professional role and task, and integrate the principles of child observation as a practice tool. The chapter also identifies the challenges which face child care social workers, who are endeavouring to keep the focus of 'the child' central to their practice, and strategies are explored, that may enable practitioners to adopt observation as a method of critical reflective practice and as a core ingredient of best practice.

A biographical note in a contemporary child care context

My interest in writing this chapter has developed over many years and integrates my diverse practice experiences having worked as a child care social worker with children and families, both in the statutory and voluntary sectors, and as a practice educator and assessor working with child care practitioners and social work candidates undergoing training. I undertook child observation training in 1992, as a lecturer, teaching on a social work qualifying programme. I observed a child over a period of a year in a private day nursery, using the Tavistock method (see Chapter 4), which included non-participant observation, recording, presentation of recordings and seminar discussion.

The learning from having undertaken this training, integrated and deepened my social work knowledge and skills, which had developed since the late 1970s, and explicitly confirmed social work values and anti-oppressive practice. Mezirow (1983) and Humphries (1988) describe the process of learning as involving 'perspective transformation'. For me, the learning from undertaking child observation training was pivotal and involved personal and professional 'perspective transformation' with respect to refocusing my practice. Humphries (1988) refers to the process of reflection, which results in perception change, as possibly revealing hidden ideologies and proposed that a supportive learning environment was essential for 'perspective transformation' to occur.

On a personal level, the impact of observing and being involved in seminar discussions, in a supportive learning environment, was highly significant. Using the Tavistock Model and method of learning provided a 'contained' time and space for 'being and not doing'. Discussions were facilitated and feelings were expertly 'held' by the facilitator, who was able to ensure that participants were 'held in mind', a process which paralleled the observers' experience with the child. To be engaged in the process of professional development and learning, without having a social work task to complete and organisational goals to meet, was refreshing and realigned my personal and professional perspectives. It enabled exploration of one's personal and professional 'self' and provided the opportunity to discover the impact of being 'alongside' a child within a 'normal' context. It also provided the opportunity to focus on the vulnerability and resilience of children and the relative powerlessness of children in a community day care setting.

It is the summation of my experience as an observer, practitioner, seminar facilitator, practice assessor and practice teacher, which has informed my perspective and contributed to my current views. The experience of observing a pre-school child was central in realigning my thinking and remains one of the most significant training and learning experiences for me over a decade later. Most recently, it has been in my role as a practice assessor with PQ candidates undertaking child observations that I have become fascinated in trying to unravel the complex and inter-dependent levels of the learning process, from a practice teaching and learning perspective and more importantly the measurable effects on practice development. How did undertaking this training affect the outcomes for children? What was the impact of using child observation as a method and how would this be received within organisations? All these questions have arisen in a climate where working within tight time frames is commonplace and where children only receive a service if they are deemed as being 'high risk and in need'.

In light of the contemporary challenges facing child care social work practitioners, enthusiasm for the benefits of child observation needs to be rooted in the realities of the practice context.

Within statutory organisations the culture of managerialism prevails and the bureau-technocrat case management approach that Pietroni-Miller (1998) identified almost a decade ago, along with the challenges it poses for practitioners to work from a provider perspective, continue to hold sway. In fact, the current situation for statutory agencies may be even more difficult than it was ten years ago, as services are targeted on the most complex cases of risk and need. Childcare practitioners spend their time managing their cases and inputting information electronically, which now takes up much of their time. Child observation training raises questions for practitioners and managers about, for example, how observation may be used as part of an assessment process. How do managers, facing the pressures of achieving performance indicators, which contribute to the star ratings within their agencies, justify the importance of being engaged in observation as a significant and important social work activity?

The potential of the child observation method lies in the important contribution it makes not only to the development of reflective and analytical child care practice, but also, to the continuous professional development of child care practitioners. Examining the evidence from the feedback from post-qualifying child care candidates endorse this claim – they consistently, and almost universally, identified the outcomes of the learning process from undertaking child observation training, as having been being highly significant. Many identified the observational skills they acquired as the most important aspect of their PQ learning. Working with PQ candidates, in post-PQ further learning forums, has served to re-enforce the importance of child observation training and its relevance for current practice. It is the significant benefits of integrating child observation within the social work role and using this as a reflective tool to inform practice and further develop professional understanding, which has provided the motivation for writing this chapter.

Before exploring in more detail the experiences of PQ candidates it is important to understand three key conceptual frameworks, already referred to, which help structure the learning that child observation elicits – reflective practice, perspective transformation and child-centred practice.

Reflective Activity

Think about your own professional journey and identify what aspect of your professional development to date – for example a theoretical framework, a piece of practice, a training event – most informs your current practice.

Three theoretical frameworks

Reflective practice

Reflecting on the messages from the inquiries into child deaths over the past four decades, it seems that little has changed. In his report following the inquiry into the death of Jasmine Beckford,

Blom Cooper (London Borough of Brent, 1985) talked about how the social worker:

> ….focused on Beverley Lavington and Morris Beckford; she averted her eyes from the children to be aware of them only as and when they were with their parents, hardly even to observe their development, and never to communicate with Jasmine on her own
>
> (Blom Cooper, 1985, cited in Trowell and Miles, 1991:51).

The more recent tragic death of Victoria Climbié painfully illustrates how, whilst changes in child care social work have and continue to take place, children are still not being adequately or accurately 'seen' or 'heard'. The child's world and the sense they make of it is not understood or even effectively described. A partial explanation for this may lie in the erosion of the traditional focus on supervision and the absence of reflective spaces, which are a prerequisite for the thoughtful, analytical practice that the Laming Inquiry (DoH, 2003) advocates (Langley, 2006; Mulcahay, 2000; Olney, 2001).

The importance of remaining close to the child requires recognising and working with the feelings stirred up in workers. Rustin (2003) and Laming (DoH, 2003) identify the detachment and inaction which affects professionals faced with emotional pain. Rustin (2003) refers to 'psychic retreats' which workers may use to defend themselves. What child observation provides is a conceptual method, which, according to Ferguson (2005), is essential when working with children who are identified as being at 'high risk' or 'in need'. He suggests that the dominance of procedurally driven practice has resulted in the emotional impact of the work being minimalised and that well-developed observational skills can act as a safeguard to this occurring.

In Chapter 4, the working definition of child observation from Ellis *et al.* (1998) described child observation as:

> *a particular way of being, an attitude and approach, which enables the worker to be responsive rather than intrusive. This involves learning how to monitor feelings and reactions and how these can inform rather than distort what is observed through the senses.*
>
> (Ellis *et al.*, 1998:21)

Integral to this definition is an understanding of the concept of reflective practice (see Chapter 3), which recognises the diverse sources of knowledge that inform practice. As an essential part of the observation process, reflective practice enables practitioners to acknowledge the actual or potential emotional impact of the observations upon them and to transfer this awareness to their practice. Boud *et al.* (1985:19) identify the importance of reflection being understood both 'intellectually and emotionally' with the likely result of it producing 'new understanding or appreciation'. An unusual feature of the observation experience is that, unlike working in a social work role, as an observer the individual is able to actively engage with the world of the child being observed and the impact this has on them personally. This involves questioning perceptions and entering a 'conversation' with personal and professional 'selves' to explore the impact of subjectivity upon professional practice. An important implication of undertaking observations, therefore, is enhanced reflective capabilities. At its most expansive, according to Peberdy (1993:47, cited in Le Riche and Tanner, 1998):

> *Observation is rather like breathing: life depends on it and we do it all the time, usually without reflection.*

For Peberdy the statement 'without reflection' implies that the process of observing and reflecting are synonymous and the two activities have become automatic professional responses that pervade all aspects of practice. If more child observation opportunities were available to qualifying and post-qualifying candidates, there is reason to believe some of the shortcomings of existing childcare practice might be addressed.

Perspective transformation

The second conceptual framework underpinning child observation is that of perspective transformation (Mezirow, 1981). The opportunity for perspective transformation is incorporated into the Tavistock method of child observation training as it provides the space to:

- Refocus on the child
- Become attuned to the child and their context
- Learn about child development
- Evaluate the impact upon 'self'
- Explore issues of discrimination and anti-oppressive practice

The observation experience encourages what Mattinson (1992) described as 'psychological distance' and this allowed for a realignment of focus, which provides an experience of the child and the child's world that is 'different'.

Integral to the teaching of child observation skills is the development of anti-oppressive and ethical practice, which is addressed by focussing on social work values, the starting point for perspective transformation. Practitioners engaged in the reflective process of learning from their observation training have the opportunity to examine their own attitudes, values and beliefs and to critically evaluate organisational practice and culture. Laying aside the task by facing the uncertainty of seeing a child on the continuum of normal development, with no particular needs, without a role or purpose was for many PQ candidates initially de-skilling. It encouraged participants to stop and 'be still', to strip away the social work role and task in order to be engaged solely in learning. Candidates found that they could immerse themselves in the process of learning and development. The change in perception involved exploration of the impact of their own subjectivity on practice and the potential for oppressive and discriminatory perspectives to prevail. Some practitioners described a process of being able to de-role and 'humanise' themselves and how they were able to become aware of their 'own' inner child, explore feelings, further develop their senses, and recognise the difference between their personal and professional perceptions. They began to examine ways in which children's rights, needs and interests are often defined by workers and the systems within their organisations and in society. As Pietroni-Miller (1998:137) states:

> One of the benefits of direct observational study is that it requires the experienced bureau-professional to explore and experiment with new perspectives by stepping outside their usual role, organisational framework and state of mind. Since this exploration takes place without everyday burdens of professional responsibility and accountability a change of perspective can safely occur.

In order to address the needs of an ethnically and culturally diverse society, however, practitioners need to be aware that:

challenge to values and views may not transform practice it might simply reinforce established ideas and preconceptions.
(Humphries, 1988:12)

For perspective transformation to be sustained practitioners require an organisational environment that encourages it through the provision of appropriate reflective forums (see Chapter 3).

Child-centred practice – 'children first'

Although, as identified earlier, the recurrence of inquiries into child care tragedies suggests there has been little change in social work practice in the past four decades, it is possible to identify some important shifts that have influenced practice. During the 1990s in response to the implementation of the Children Act 1989 and government research initiatives (DoH, 1995) there was a refocussing in child care social work towards more child-centred and needs-led approaches. Following these changes the introduction of the Framework for Assessment in 2000 (DoH, 2000) realigned social workers thinking to encompass ecological and strengths-based approaches to working with children and their families. Post-Climbié, the Every Child Matters agenda (DFES, 2004) and the Children Act 2004 have placed children at the centre of child care practice across the welfare sector, with universal services for children linked to a qualification and a standards-based framework which is outcome-based.

As a result of these progressive changes social work interventions have become more purposeful, child focused and linked to formalised plans and outcomes. In some settings social workers have been supported to undertake direct work with children to refocus on listening to children and keeping the child central to the work – being able to hold the individual child 'in mind' and to see the 'child first', within the continuum of child development. The change from perceiving the child solely as a child 'at risk' or 'in need' has been crucial. This emphasis and perspective has required practitioners to engage with the child as an individual with a unique heritage, culture and ethnicity and has been central to seeing the 'whole child' and its perception of the world.

Child observation has been used by practitioners to reconfigure their practice, to assist them in focussing on the whole child and to help them identify strengths in children and their social networks. The method is a significant feature of the process of assessment as it assists practitioners in identifying needs, interests, wishes and risks and in learning about the individual child. Trowell and Miles (1991) and Rustin (1989) refer to observation as an evolving experience in which a picture emerges not only of the child, but also of the relationships and interactions between the child and her carers. The cultural context and the environment influence the observation and the observer's experience of it. By emphasising the importance of observation in child-centred assessments, it also highlights assessment as a process and not an event, and challenges policymakers to consider what are realistic timeframes for the completion of such assessments.

With these three conceptual frameworks in place, candidates undertaking child observation are well placed to create a continuous professional development profile that ensures their practice remains child-centred, reflective and ethical. The following section explores the rich learning of the candidates from their observational experiences.

Learning points

- Child observation has the potential to shape both the personal and professional development of practitioners.
- Reflective practice is integral to child observation and both informs it and is informed by it.
- Practitioners undertaking child observation often experience significant shifts in their professional perspectives.
- Child observation encourages child-centred professional practice.

Reflective Activity

- Which of the three theoretical perspectives outlined above do you find most helpful for your practice and why?

The observational experiences and practice-related learning of PQ candidates

From examining the Child Observation Unit assignments and portfolio material that PQ candidates have produced, it has been possible to draw out a number of recurrent themes:

- Doing and being – learning to 'be' in order to 'do'
- Attunement – learning to see the child and how this links with child development
- Dealing with the emotional pain
- Power issues and anti-oppressive and ethical practice
- Integrating observation into the organisational context

Doing and being – learning to 'be' in order to 'do'

Fawcett (1996) refers to observation as being:

> *A kind of perceptive watching, and informed way of looking that raises awareness and sharpens understanding. It helps to bring to notice what would otherwise be overlooked … we all have a tendency to see what we are looking for and to look for what we know about. Rarely do we take the time to stop and watch intently.*
>
> (Fawcett, 1996:6)

It is remarkably difficult to slow down and leave activities and outcomes to one side. Candidates within the child observation seminar groups talked about the desire to be 'doing' and the difficulty of putting the task to one side, deroling and staying with the process of learning.

When beginning my observations I found myself feeling confused. Although I knew I had no assessment to carry out and the nursery didn't have expectations for me to undertake any tasks, I found myself thinking I was under prepared.

(PQ candidate)

Observation is challenging: the observer has to constantly clear out other thoughts from their mind in order to become interested and receptive.

(PQ candidate)

'Doing' in seminar conversations appeared in many guises for candidates:

- The challenge of stopping another activity to prioritise getting to an observation session as timetabled
- Managing to let go of a 'doing' agenda during the observation when an incomplete task 'back in the office' or personal issue is preoccupying and distracting from the observation
- Learning to resist 'doing' something during the observation, for example, either being tempted to take notes in order to 'look busy' or to initiate an interaction with a child

The difficulty of unreservedly 'keeping the child in mind' has become very apparent to me throughout the observations I undertook. Despite being a relatively small nursery, the distractions and noise at times caused considerable difficulties in maintaining a vigilant observation of the specific child. Beyond this I was aware of the need to completely clear my mind of any personal issues which might have an impact on my observations in order to completely focus and be in tune with this child and their world.

(PQ candidate)

The different types of 'doing' diminish the quality of the observation being undertaken as the observer is not fully attentive to what they are watching and their responses to it. Candidates, however, evidenced that through experiencing the observer role their ability to refrain from 'doing' grew.

The child observation module presented an opportunity to stand back from interaction and withhold judgement, to practice maintaining a presence and concentration on a single subject without doing anything.

(PQ candidate)

Child observation was a psychological and emotional exercise that touched the personal and professional parts of me and made me realize how little I observe, adequately grasp the essence of children and capture and hold them in mind as the primary focus, primary client and fundamental reason I became a social worker.

(PQ candidate)

The 'perspective transformation', referred to earlier, that child observation promotes is of particular relevance to this aspect of learning and practice and professional development. For one candidate the shift in her perception of her professional role and behaviour was vividly conveyed in her assignment.

At the very time I should have been observing to see what children are really experiencing within a home or a family in order that I could address the real issues, I have instead interfered and changed the dynamics, thus omitting my ability to accurately assess.

(PQ candidate)

'Being not doing' in order to 'do' – to practice more effectively – was experienced as highly significant learning, as candidates felt able to explore the impact upon the 'self' of what was being observed. This process resulted in an exploration of the impact of perception and a focus upon 'difference', when undertaking the recording of the observations.

> *I found that these sessions were, at this point in my professional development a great luxury, in that they allowed me to concentrate on a much narrower range of issues than I normally would do in my work. Focusing on one child took a certain amount of practice and mental energy. The observation was not one-dimensional; sometimes during the observation, and more frequently afterwards, I was very conscious of my own position and feelings, and I felt a sense of permission to spend time not only thinking of the child, but about myself and why I am where I am.*
>
> (PQ candidate)

The sharing of different perspectives and perceptions within the seminar group provided an opportunity to explore the effects of power imbalance and cultural and gender difference. The group process provided a dynamic, whereby recording, reflection and inquiry could be achieved, without candidates feeling they had to interpret and make judgements. In addition, the seminar format freed them from having to know answers. Letting go of the role of social work practitioner provided the space to observe the child and enter the process of reflective enquiry. The qualitative evaluation from candidates identified how the process realigned their focus on the child and this resulted in them becoming 'attuned' to the child's world. In particular candidates identified the seminar group experience as a safe learning environment where feelings, questions and reflections could be 'contained'. Candidates, particularly, commented upon having permission to stay with their observations and the material this generated, without the requirement of having to interpret what was observed. The structure and boundaries of the seminar groups confirmed and reinforced the observations, by ensuring the focus remained with the child.

Staying with the observations was an important skill to develop given the emotional impact of the work, which was acknowledged within the seminar discussions. The significance of this skill development cannot be underestimated, given the prevailing emphasis within contemporary practice towards higher risk cases, action and outcomes, which can result in insufficient attention being paid to the child's experience (Cooper, 2005; Ferguson, 2005; Rustin, 2004). The observation experience afforded opportunity for candidates to question and challenge themselves personally and professionally. Practitioners were able to be 'still' and stay with uncertainty, which left them able to enter the child's world.

> *Through the observation process, I have learnt to step back more often and observe without being tempted to intervene immediately. The capacity to draw back and to reflect and think while events are unfolding enables learning to take place in a way that allows thoughtless action to become thoughtful.*
>
> (PQ candidate)

The overwhelming feedback from PQ Child Care candidates is of the importance of having a 'protected space'. The opportunity to be, to focus, to question and reflect were cited as some of the most significant learning processes arising from the observation experience.

Attunement – learning to see the child and how this links with child development

Universally, candidates identified that the observation experience resulted in them being able to realign themselves with the child. Refocusing on the continuum of normal child development enabled candidates to focus on a child's strengths and recognise the ages and stages of child development and the risk of adult perspectives influencing assessments.

> *I found the observation experience invaluable in focusing on the individual child and this enabled the practitioner to overcome the hurdle inherent in the process of adults undertaking child assessment.*
>
> (PQ candidate)

The importance of 'play' in child development was recognised and many candidates were surprised to discover the range of behaviours, within the stages of development, which would be considered as 'normal'. There was consideration about how expressive and imaginative play, taken out of context, could be misinterpreted and candidates universally identified the importance of not labelling children.

> *Fundamentally undertaking child observations provided the time to think about the child and to really consider the importance of keeping the child in mind and also provided the opportunity to reflect upon children's relative powerlessness.*
>
> (PQ candidate)

Through the observation process candidates were able to recognise how it encouraged them to question their assumptions, perceptions and practice when, for example, they might be completing an assessment. Undertaking observations over a period of time, emphasised the danger of making 'snap-shot' judgements about children. Many identified that in practice they had made assumptions and judgements about children based on a minimal number of visits, which were 'skewed' and did not accurately reflect the child's strengths, developmental status or needs. Candidates identified that one of the dangers of working with children who may be at high risk and in need was the tendency to focus their attention upon 'deficits' as opposed to 'strengths'. Some emphasised the importance of repeating the experience of child observation over time, to ensure realignment' with the 'whole' child.

> *I also found it useful to observe 'J' at different times of the day…they may be hungry, tired or distracted in some way, potentially, all of these issues could impact on what the observer sees.*
>
> (PQ candidate)

In relation to working with disabled children in particular, child observation was seen for some as being a vital skill to gain understanding of children's individual ways of communicating. Again the concept of seeing the 'child first' was highlighted as often missing from childcare practice, when so much attention is given to the adult agendas. With the introduction of the common Assessment Framework (CAF) under the Every Child Matters agenda, this is the time to focus on the 'whole' child. As part of the multi-professional CAF team, the specialist childcare social worker needs to ensure the child is the focus and it is the child's 'voice' that is heard. Child observation provides a useful source of information for assessment and helps to identify the child's strengths, cultural and ethnic background, interests, needs and any risks, within an ecological framework. Two candidates succinctly captured this key learning point:

> *In short, the child is 're-centred' by the experience of observation and I have found this a salutary prompt to inform my practice.*
>
> (PQ candidate)

> *Observation really gave me an experience of the child that stayed with me in a way that I can only liken to how memories remain with us in life, for example, after a holiday…we carry with us the memory of moments in which we stopped, absorbed our surroundings, took a mental picture and formed an emotional attachment to an experience*
>
> (PQ candidate)

Dealing with the emotional pain

Since the tragic death of Victoria Climbié there has been a resurgence in interest in the lack of attention paid in social work practice to the emotional dimensions of the work (Cooper, 2005; Ferguson, 2005; Rustin, 2004). For Rustin there is a clear, albeit dangerous, rationale, for the desire of 'professionals to keep a distance from the intense feelings stirred up by exposure to human cruelty and madness' (Rustin, 2003:1). In her analysis of the critical moments in Victoria Climbié's life, Rustin writes about the feelings of the workers involved:

> *The feelings aroused in doing this difficult work are hard to make space for. They are uncomfortable, and they are liable to cause trouble in the sense of demanding more thought and more work if taken seriously. They are 'gut feelings' referred to by one witness who spoke about how these feelings got put to one side rather than be the subject of reflection and evaluation.*
>
> Rustin (2004:13)

Rustin (2004) identified that a failure to address the powerful emotions, which can be the result of working with violence and abuse, can result in workers and their organisation 'mirroring' the behaviour of those accessing the services:

> *Instead of being able to observe and thus question Kouao's belief system, workers began to mirror it.*
>
> (Rustin, 2004:3)

It is evident that social workers find the need to defend themselves against the emotional pain of the children with whom they worked. Ferguson (2005), however, proposes that addressing the emotional impact on staff undertaking the work is not on the agenda for most organisations and he suggests that in the process of dominant procedural responses:

> *Attention to the psychological and emotional aspects of doing social work and child protection has largely been ignored and squeezed out.*
>
> Ferguson (2005:781)

PQ candidates clearly valued child observation as a means of enabling them to safely stay in touch with this level of emotional pain. Several candidates recognised Rustin's (2004) description of the fear of contamination, which plays a huge part in the way the worker and organisations behave. Child observation seminars provide a 'safe container' and vehicle for sharing feelings and thoughts about what the observation had triggered for the practitioner. The emotional impact of the work cannot be underestimated. Enabling workers to listen to their feelings and safely explore the impact the work has upon them, was identified as essential for safe and 'best 'practice and candidates identified child observation was seen as a significant and a core method which could achieve this.

> *I found the seminar experience particularly useful to 'safely' discuss feelings/fears, which my observations generated, and the feedback I received which made a definite contribution to my development/my being able to challenge some of my oppressive thinking. I especially valued being 'heard' and will ensure I afford those I work with the time to be heard.*
>
> (PQ candidate)

In several assignments candidates cited how the case management approach was being utilised within organisations at the expense of encouraging reflective opportunities to critically analyse practice issues. Langley's (2006) research identified that generally supervision was not being used to explore the impact of the work upon practitioners and this left staff feeling unsupported with the complex and qualitative aspects of the work. Candidates universally identified child observation as being one method, which could encourage critical, analytical and reflective practice. One candidate captured this in her reference to how:

> *The act of permitting free thought and emotion exposes what can motivate or inhibit professional judgement.*
>
> (PQ candidate)

Power issues and anti-oppressive and ethical practice

In many respects the learning related to anti-oppressive and ethical issues was inextricably linked to candidates' realigned practice, which they recognised to be more child-centred. Issues of power and powerlessness were a constant thread throughout the observation experience. For one candidate observing a child is a way of:

> *bluntly reminding the worker of the power that they hold and also in terms of exposing the worker to the vulnerability of the child to the actions and the attitudes of the adults around them.*
>
> (PQ candidate)

Some candidates, for example, struggled with the issue of whether they should obtain the child's consent to be observed, which did not routinely occur, as it was the parent's decision whether to give their consent and whether they wished their child to know about the observation. This linked to practitioners examining the way they approached and communicated with children in their work. For most practitioners, the learning from undertaking child observation as a 'candidate', though uncomfortable initially, enabled them to look closely at their attitudes, values and beliefs and the impact this had on their personal and professional perceptions. For example, the child chosen for them may not have been the one they would have chosen to observe. The choices made by or for candidates encouraged them to think about how some children get overlooked and are not 'seen' and this led them on to reviewing their practice with children.

Having the time to observe also heightened candidates' awareness of the context in which children find themselves. Candidates exploring the impact of children's experience within day care settings identified positive for some pre-school children, but also recognised more clearly the powerlessness of this group of children.

> *It occurred to me that as a child in a playgroup situation she did not have the power to challenge or question my presence. However, I remained uncomfortable with the concept of power imbalance, and no doubt will make efforts in future practice to consider and minimise the effects as much as possible.*
>
> (PQ candidate)

In addition, candidates identified that often group care contexts were lacking positive models of cultural, social and ethnic diversity. Several male candidates explored the impact upon children of having few, if any, male role models within the day care and pre-school education system and their own feelings of discomfort as a man in the observer role.

Alongside their heightened awareness of the potential for oppressive practice, candidates developed an enhanced understanding of reflective practice. Candidates became more aware of how reflective practice contributes to higher standards and becomes empowering practice, whilst simultaneously enabling workers to effectively manage the responsibility, authority and duty vested in the specialist social work role and task. An unexpected outcome of this heightened awareness is discussed below in relation to the organisational context of practice. What this development underlines is that through the child observation experience candidate's awareness of oppression was not only enhanced with regard to children, but also in relation to their own professional experiences.

Integrating observation into the organisational context

Two recurrent themes that were evident in the child observation assignments and the evaluation of the experience were the enthusiasm of candidates to integrate their experiences of doing child observation into their everyday practice and secondly, the challenges they identified from within the organisational context to achieving this. For many of the candidates undertaking child observations was a refreshing reminder of why they had entered the social work profession. Unit evaluation comments identified that practitioners had refocused their professional approach and child observation training enabled them to integrate messages from research, theory, legislation and policy affecting children and families directly into practice. For some candidates, they identified a growth in confidence as they acknowledged the powerful effect the training had had upon them. The feedback from candidates identified the positive promotion of childcare values within the training, which resulted in promoting the rights and needs of children.

Some candidates identified examples of how their practice had incorporated child observation. One candidate, for example, requested a delay in care proceedings to carry out an observation on a child and to submit the recordings as evidence. Another candidate made a proposal for a change in agency policy with respect to the training for potential adoptive parents, which was accepted in their agency.

> *Adoption teams are currently being encouraged to involve prospective adopters in Sure Start nurseries, to gain hands on work with children.*
>
> (PQ candidate)

In addition to the candidate-led changes in practice, there was an expressed desire for managers to recognise the significance of 'therapeutic' work with children and the essential part child observation had to play in facilitating this. Candidates particularly commented upon the importance of using the method in the assessment process, as it emphasises an ecological approach and a 'strengths' perspective. Further applications for the use of child observation as a method were identified and emphasised by practitioners, for example, the use of observational recordings in care proceedings, and generally, in reports for court.

> *It was not too long before I was giving evidence in court proceedings. The counsel for the defence, who was clearly aware of the National Assessment Framework…asked me to define child observation. I have never been more grateful to have also done my homework on this subject. I answered him confidently and knowledgably. Thank you PQ2.*
>
> (PQ candidate)

Child observation could be used within a whole range of assessments, for example, reports for approving foster carers; linking reports in adoption; attachment assessments; parenting skills assessments, and when reviewing, monitoring and developing care plans. The use of recording was also seen as having wider implications, when working in partnership with parents and carers.

An interesting and perhaps unexpected outcome of candidates taking part in the observation process was their determination to challenge established organisational practices, which in the light of their refocused and realigned child-centred practice were no longer deemed acceptable. From engaging in the child observation process, candidates felt better equipped to challenge 'the system' and found that their learning reinforced the child care values requirements and the GSCC code of practice. This personal and professional realignment was identified as giving practitioners 'strength and courage' to uphold best practice.

From their experience of the child observation seminars, many candidates confirmed the importance of having safe and thoughtful forums and were eager to create opportunities for case discussions within their organisations, where groups of practitioners could present cases and explore, discuss and share the issues as a routine part of practice. Whilst it was recognised that such a change within organisations would require a huge cultural shift, candidates could see the potential benefits, as the existence of such forums could contribute to the development of a culture of collective responsibility for practice interventions, and for the outcomes for children. Waiting for evidence to emerge to hold a child protection inquiry should not be the only space for this type of shared approach. This was seen to be particularly important with the development of the new integrated teams within Children's Services and for inter-professional practice to thrive.

In many of the candidates 'Final Evaluations of Learning', which went into their practice portfolios, child observation was seen by many as being the most significant source of learning whilst on the PQ programme. This candidate's comment highlights how child observation skills grow over time:

On leaving the playgroup I practically ran to the car to make key word notes, however as I began to write, a picture came of the action which surprised me in its detail. This has got sharper with each successive session.

(PQ candidate)

Many identified an interest in having further opportunities to observe children over a longer period, suggesting it needs to be a central thread in CPD initiatives.

Child observation is, on the basis of the evidence above, a method of practice that has serious implications for the organisations responsible for delivering child care services. Candidates identified how they struggled working as a 'bureau-technocrat', spending large amounts of time inputting information electronically, dealing with finances and ensuring targets, which linked with agency performance indicators, were met. For most this was not the profession they had trained for and whilst recognising the importance of accurate recording and effective data management, they questioned the rationale for squeezing out the specialist provider knowledge and skills, which are required for safe and 'best practice'. Candidates expressed concern that in their experience organisations would regard child observation as a luxury and not a core skill and requirement, for example, in the process of assessment.

An additional organisational consideration is the move to inter-professional work contexts. Candidates' experiences of child observation suggest it could be used as a collective professional 'tool' to enable different professional bodies to develop a 'common language', which could be used in assessment processes and procedures, and within the development of services for all children. Working within integrated teams, childcare social workers need to be confident in their professional role and task and work explicitly within the social work code of practice and with the specialist values requirements, central to their practice. Using this method has demonstrated that it assists practitioners to be confident and competent in using their knowledge base and skills, through applying thoughtful and critically reflective approaches. They are more able to address the complex and stressful issues, which face them routinely in practice, working with children and young people.

If organisations are to take child observation seriously it requires appropriate resourcing, which would as a minimum require practitioners to have access to a form of supervision not dissimilar to the seminar group. The demise of reflective forms of supervision, which extends beyond case management, is well documented (Olney, 2001; Mulcahy, 2000), but it was precisely this type of support that candidates valued highly in undertaking their child observation. Candidates lamented the way that for most practitioners, supervision in organisations has become a management tool that focused on the management of the workloads and recording outcomes. Qualitative supervision, which critically analyses casework issues, has for the most part been squeezed out of line management accountability (see Chapter 3). Pressures on middle managers to produce results and provide performance indicators to track outcomes for children has had positive results by ensuring that children do not 'get lost' in the system, but whilst children do not 'get lost' sometimes the professional needs of practitioners do.

Social workers working with high-risk situations must be well informed and have a high level of ethical, critical and analytical skills to be able to practice effectively. The question raised for organisations and practitioners is how this can be achieved within the existing framework of support and supervision. Child observation is one effective method which could contribute to 'best practice' that focuses on children.

Reflective Activity

Think about the children and young people you are currently working with and consider which of the five experiences identified by PQ candidates most resonates with your professional experiences.

Learning points

- Learning to 'be' as well as 'do' is an important aspect of professional development that arises from undertaking child observations.
- Practitioners engaging in child observations experience heightened awareness of the needs of children and the emotional pain surrounding their circumstances.
- Power issues come to the fore through observing children.
- Employers need to facilitate opportunities for practitioners to undertake observations.

Conclusion

Peberdy's reference to observation as being 'rather like breathing' (1993, cited in Le Riche and Tanner, 1998) powerfully illustrates the taken-for-granted, but essential, qualities of observation. The evidence of candidates' learning that forms the body of this chapter endorses this view – for many candidates the experience of doing child observation helped them breathe again when they had felt stifled by organisational cultures and contexts, whose defining systems were the antithesis of the characteristics of observational contexts.

Child observation has a significant part to play in reducing the risk of further tragedies occurring from child deaths at the hands of adult carers and in developing services that are more responsive to the needs of all children. It is significant in addressing the subjectivity involved in assessment and is an important method to be used as part of a preventative, holistic service that will promote the five principles of Every Child Matters, the Children Act 2004, the National Services Framework for Children and the Youth Green Paper (2006).

Currently, the plea from childcare practitioners is the need to be supported to have the time to undertake planned, responsive and effective work. This would require a restructuring of how a professional childcare social worker's time should be spent. If the emphasis is placed on improving outcomes, rather than a case management approach, then a different way of practicing could re-emerge. Ensuring that evaluative reflective practice is routinely part of undertaking complex assessments and planning for children may require a wholesale change in organisational practice in

Children's Services. Evidence from the inquiries into child deaths, PQ candidates and feedback from children themselves would support this change.

The success of good practice should be celebrated and strategies need to be developed that ensure staff are properly trained, supported and valued. If organisations become more open to discussing dilemmas, fears and the needs of workers, then children might be better protected and empowered, and their views heard more readily. Organisations have to be ready to see 'what is in front of their eyes' and to avoid the prevalence of 'organisational defensiveness'.

The emphasis within the observation method on reflective practice is a significant way in which we can bear witness to the strengths, needs, interests and wishes of children, to make positive change, which could improve outcomes and promote development. Organisations that fail to grasp this opportunity for enhancing ethical and reflective practice and dismiss observation as 'a luxury' are taking risks with their staff and, more worryingly, heighten the risk to the children they seek to safeguard.

Chapter summary

- Child observation has considerable potential to transform practitioner perspectives and to promote reflective, ethical, child-centred practice.
- The learning and professional development acquired by candidates is rich and multi-faceted and includes heightened awareness of and attunement to children's developmental stages and needs; greater understanding of the impact of context on children's behaviour and development; and deeper recognition of the extent of oppression in the lives of children.
- Child observations impact on personal and professional identities and understanding and require supportive learning contexts for it's potential to be maximised.
- Child observation has an essential role in an integrated Children's Services.

Reflective questions

In what way does child observation help to focus on the child?

How does child observation contribute to understanding of 'normal' child development?

What can be learnt from undertaking child observation about the importance of providing reflective spaces for practitioners?

How does child observation contribute to reflective and analytical practice?

Notes

1. This chapter is dedicated to Val Jones who was committed to ensuring that child observation was an integral part of the practice and taught curriculum on qualifying and post-qualifying training.
2. With thanks to the candidates in the 2004 PQ cohort for their generosity in sharing their learning, and for consenting to their material being included in this chapter.

Chapter 9

'Holding the child in mind': working in partnership with children, their families, carers and professionals

Gillian Ruch

Chapter learning aims

- To identify and apply, in a critical and reflective way, theoretical perspectives and methods of intervention appropriate to partnership-based practice with children, families, carers and professionals
- To enhance practitioners' awareness of the emotionally demanding nature of working with children, families, carers and professionals
- To encourage the development of a critically reflective understanding of effective, empowering and ethical methods of working with children, families, carers and wider communities

Introduction

The title of this chapter derives from the public inquiry into the death of Kimberley Carlile – *A Child in Mind* (Blom-Cooper *et al.*, 1987). The phrase 'holding the child in mind' summed up one of the primary concerns of the inquiry report – the inability of professionals to sustain a focus on the needs of the child in complex and emotionally charged situations. Sadly, this was not an isolated incident and the misdirected attention of social workers and other professionals is a recurrent feature of many inquiries into child deaths (Reder and Duncan, 2004), including the Laming Inquiry Report (DoH, 2003) into the death of Victoria Climibié. Nor, however, is simply focussing on the child an effective solution to the challenges of childcare social work practice. All children are situated in social networks comprised of their birth families and/or substitute carers (with children known to social workers frequently straddling both of these groups) and the professionals involved with them and their family. Any work undertaken with a child, therefore, even if done on an individual basis, needs to acknowledge and integrate the child's external world into the work.

Within child care social work practice there is a growing concern about an increasing emphasis on narrow definitions of what it means to 'do' social work and what constitutes an effective outcome (Charles, 2004). To counter this trend this chapter is structured in two specific ways. First, it provides brief outlines of theoretical frameworks for 'thinking about doing' social work to ensure practice is not engaged with thoughtlessly or reactively simply to meet organisational requirements. The distinctive characteristics of the chosen theoretical frameworks are their emphasis on partnership in practice and the importance of practitioners intervening with a reflective stance that acknowledges the significance of 'self' in social work practice. Secondly, it explores some specific theoretically informed skills and techniques for working with children, young people and their caring networks. It is hoped that practitioners who have acquired this combination of theoretically informed thinking and doing will be able to practice in reflective and effective ways that are capable of responding to the complexities and challenges of contemporary practice.

The first challenge for child care social work practitioners is to hold the tension between the needs of the child and the circumstances of the child's family. The inability or difficulty for social workers to 'hold the child in mind' is directly related to the social defences against anxiety, discussed in Chapter 4. The reflective approaches identified in this earlier chapter are crucial, therefore, for work with children and young people and for identifying relevant responses and interventions. Practitioners must have an awareness of the impact of the work on their professional capabilities. Bowlby (1988) coined the phrase a 'secure base' to describe the foundations required for the healthy emotional development of children. Practitioners also need such a 'secure base', to ensure they can sustain their ability to engage in effective and ethical practice. On the post-qualification programme practitioners are part of action learning sets and have the experience of taking part in case discussions. One practitioner in her assignment articulated how important these discussion groups were for allowing her to express and explore the emotional responses she had to a case:

> … I quietly owned I felt a sense of relief that I was not going to have to have any direct contact with this family, whose violent tentacles stretched out endlessly. I felt guilty about such anxiety, hence it was with a sense of relief this area was openly acknowledged in the Unit … This process helped me own the issue of working with anxiety and fear; the emotions it fosters within my professional practice and the support needed but often not available. This could not have happened had the group not been collaborative supportive and willing to expose our own limitations and mistakes, plus the ability to say 'I don't know.' It offered a sense of being held, which enabled me to acknowledge more openly the dynamics of my work on a personal and professional level.

A professional 'secure base' is comprised of organisational contexts that recognise the demanding nature of the work undertaken and which, as a direct consequence of this understanding, provide accessible and relevant support systems. With these foundations in place the opportunity to promote positive change in partnership with children, young people and their families is increased.

Working with children and young people with complex and additional needs, whether this is due to disability, abuse, or geographical dislocation, conferring on them asylum seeker or refugee status is painful.

Effective practice capable of promoting positive change, however, is dependent on practitioners remaining open to the pain of the child or young person. To do this practitioners need support. This is the bottom line for effective work with children and young people. Without support practitioners will not hear what is being communicated. They will not be as effective as they could be. In a recent consultation exercise with service users about the content of post-qualifying social work programmes, the service user representatives clearly and forcefully articulated their concern about their inconsistent experiences of practitioners, who are either inexplicably replaced due to organisational imperatives or are absent through stress-related illness. For these individuals, a sustained and consistent relationship with a social worker was one of their top priorities and in their view central to effective interventions and outcomes. They were eager to emphasise that continuing professional development programmes need to enable practitioners to challenge organisational systems and expectations that prohibit the development of meaningful service user–practitioner relationships. Ensuring appropriate support systems are in place to facilitate such professional relationships is a prerequisite for effective work with children, young people and their carers. Throughout the chapter the reader is invited to reflect on how they are supported in their practice (with reference to Chapter 4) and what forms of support they can identify that would further enhance their practice.

Systemic work with families, carers and professionals

Theoretical underpinnings

Systemic approaches in social work practice have developed considerably in recent years with a shift in terminology from family therapy to systemic practice reflecting the broader application of systems theory to all social networks and not simply families. Systemic therapy is informed by social constructionist theory and post-modernism. In essence these theoretical positions consider there is no one universal truth and that individuals experiences are constructed through language from their personal experiences and relationships, thereby creating multiple truths/realities. The key characteristics of contemporary systemic therapy according to Dallos and Draper (2000) are:

- Realities are multiple and socially constructed
- Individual behaviours are social and inter-personal, influenced and informed by wider systems – family, community, society – and multitude of factors – personal, cultural, societal, political
- Meanings are jointly constructed through the dynamic processes of conversations
- Focus on orientations to systemic work rather than techniques, e.g. reflecting teams/conversations; collaborative approach and role of non-expert therapist; narrative therapies; externalising problems
- Recognition of power dynamics and structural/cultural obstacles to equality

In contemporary social work practice the shift to systemic approaches is of particular significance for several reasons. First, with the imminent merging of social work and education services and the closer integration with health service provision, practitioners are spending increasing amounts of their time engaged with colleagues in inter-professional dialogue, discussion and decision-making. The differing views on appropriate interventions and potential for professional disagreement and discord necessitates practitioners attending to professional dynamics as well as family dynamics. Systemic thinking is extremely helpful in this regard. The importance of attending to professional issues is even greater when the scope for mirroring of family dynamics within professionals systems, known as 'conflict by proxy' (Furniss, 1991), is recognised. Secondly, the fundamental principles of systemic thinking place value on each individual's experiences, views and perspectives on the situations causing concern. Integral, therefore, to systemic approaches is recognition of the importance of hearing the voices of the service users and carers and of valuing difference and diversity both within and between family systems. Thirdly, in what can feel at times like an 'evidence-driven' culture, which risks over-simplifying the social difficulties practitioners encounter, the inclusive and ecological characteristics of systemic perspectives ensure there is no swift recourse to simplistic solutions to complex and multi-faceted situations. Given the type of social challenges social workers encounter it is crucial they are not under the illusion that they can resolve them in a straightforward manner. Most of the children and young people that the PQ framework refers to as having 'additional and complex needs' find themselves in this situation because of a host of inter-dependent factors – individual, familial and societal – which, therefore, in order to be alleviated require thoughtful and multi-faceted responses.

Two useful methods for exploring systemic ideas in professional development and practice contexts that demonstrate the inclusive, respectful, thoughtful and empowering qualities of this theoretical perspective are sculpting exercises and reflective conversations.

Family and professional sculpts

The process of building a sculpt was devised by Duhl *et al.* (1973) and involves individuals from a family, team or other group context physically expressing their inter-relationships by positioning themselves in relation to each other. Papp *et al.* (1973:199) who refer to sculpting as a form of choreography, highlighting its dynamic as opposed to rigid quality, describe it as a way of enabling 'vague impressions and confused feelings on the periphery of awareness' to be 'given form through spatial expression'. For Geddes and Medway (1978:219) a sculpt is 'a symbolic non-verbal activity that often serves as a stimulus to non-verbal interchange' and can encompass visual, symbolic and sensory forms of communication. Sculpts can be likened to three-dimensional ecomaps as they throw light on how relationships have become entrenched and family or professional dysfunction has arisen. As with ecomaps, sculpts can have a powerful affective impact. In the process of developing a sculpt, the emotional interaction and relationships between family members and professionals can be starkly visually represented. Spaces, splits, alliances, attitudes and underlying features of relationships become visible.

Doing a sculpt

In continuing professional development contexts (within teams or in externally organised professional development events) the sculpting exercise is undertaken in two stages – the first stage sculpts family members and the second sculpts professionals. The practitioner concerned with the case presents the broad details and current situation. Small groups of practitioners (3–4) within the team/training group are asked to think about the position of a particular family member in the scenario outlined. One by one a representative from each group, guided by their small group colleagues, positions themselves in relation to other members of the family system and adopts a pose that reflects their feelings about their position. As they do so each person is asked to explain why they have placed themselves as they have. As the sculpt develops, previously positioned individuals may wish to re-adjust their position. On completion of the first stage of a sculpt the participants are invited to express what they feel about the overall systemic representation. The observing small group members are also invited to participate in the discussion. The same process is then repeated with each small group considering the position of one of the professionals engaged with the family and depicting this in a sculpt of the professional system.

The following example of a sculpt undertaken by a group of practitioners on a post-qualification programme illustrates the sculpting process and its effectiveness. The case material is of a hypothetical family but draws on a range of professional experiences.

Family Details   Kelly is 14 and living in a residential children's home in the same town as her mother, Karen and younger siblings – Marie aged 10 and Sean aged 2. Kelly was sexually abused by her birth father, who no longer lives at home but has contact with the younger siblings. Karen has a new partner, Mike, who has recently moved into the family home.

Sculpt – Phase One   During the first sculpt of the family it immediately became apparent how Karen was positioned so that she could only see her new partner. Kelly was at considerable distance on the other side of the room with obstacles (chairs, tables etc.) between her and her family but was looking in their direction. Marie was behind her mother, looking down, holding Sean's hand. Sean was at his mother's feet – close to her but not in her line of vision. Mike was positioned half in and half out of the doorway looking towards Karen. Kelly's father, Gary, was placed in the far corner of the room with his arm stretched outwards Marie and Sean.

The positions adopted reflected how the different small groups responded to the information provided by the group facilitator. The overwhelming impression arising from the sculpt, for the participants and observers, was how Karen had an impossible task trying to keep all three of her children within view at the same time. Kelly appeared estranged and distant from her family despite her orientation towards them. Marie and Sean's positions were equally poignant and informative as both were physically close to their mother but neither of them were receiving attention from her. Sean was present but invisible and Marie appeared to be cutting out any connections with other family members, apart from Sean. In response to the sculpt, one practitioner holding a similar case commented on how it accurately captured her sense of the family's dynamics. In particular she found the affective comments and emotional responses of those involved in the sculpt itself and those observing group members helped her understand better what the individuals in the family she was working with might be experiencing.

Sculpt – Phase Two   In the second stage of the exercise the professional system was sculpted. The person representing the caseholding social worker positioned himself in a similar way to Karen, central to all the other family members but unable to have them all in his view simultaneously. The challenge for Karen to 'hold in mind' all her children, illustrated in the family sculpt, was replicated in the professional sculpt. The difficulty one social worker has addressing the diverse needs of several children in one family was immediately apparent. The social worker was joined by the health visitor, who stood shoulder to shoulder with him and indicated she was 'sheltering under his wing'. The health visitor representative said she would provide factual information, e.g. percentile chart figures etc. but was relying on the social worker to make all the difficult professional decisions. Not unlike Sean's position, the health visitor was connected in a minimal way to the wider system. The health visitor's dependence on the social worker and 'fear' of becoming more involved in the messy, inter-subjective aspects of the case reflected Sean's uncertainty about what was going on and his insecure, 'fearful' dependence on his mother. Sean was physically connected to his mother, as the health visitor was to the social worker, but neither Sean nor the health visitor were affectively or 'meaningfully' connected. The residential social worker representative positioned herself, without hesitation, at a distance from the social worker-health visitor dyad. The mirroring of this position with Kelly's was immediately apparent and highlighted how overlooked and undervalued residential workers often feel. This was reinforced by a 'real' residential social worker in the group who identified entirely with this marginalised position and systemic representation. Gary's probation officer similarly mirrored Gary's position – connected to the family but at a distance. The representative emphasised that her focus was on Gary and that she did not wish to get involved in ongoing child protection concerns.

Observing the professional sculpt clearly illustrated the impact of the different professional remits and priorities on inter-professional relationships and practice. The sculpting exercise helped to make sense of the difficulties that can arise in engaging with other professionals and to understand what can appear to be a professional's ambivalent attitudes to involvement. This is of particular importance for social work practitioners who so often feel that they are left to 'carry the can.' Sculpts highlight why these feelings exist and where they come from. With this level of information and insight social work practitioners are equipped to respond differently and not succumb to the 'victim role' as is all too often the case. In this case, the sculpt highlighted how providing a co-worker could be a potentially effective way of helping the social worker respond to the multifaceted needs of different family members.

An important caveat on the use of sculpts is the recognition that they do not represent 'the truth' of the situation. From systemic and social constructivist perspectives 'truth' is always constructed, dynamic and situated. Sculpts do not licence practitioners to tell the family or other professionals that there is a definitive explanation for and solution to their situation. Rather sculpts can inform further dialogue between individuals. Whilst sculpts are most commonly used in professional contexts they can be used creatively with families. 'Feeling stuck' with families and colleagues is an all too familiar experience for social work practitioners. Sculpts are one means of potentially exploring 'stuck' situations and looking for alternative approaches. Encouraging families to visually express their inter-relationships can offer individuals different perspectives on entrenched patterns of behaviour and be a catalyst to relate in new ways.

Learning points

- Individual positions are constructed in relation to others.
- Sculpt are an inclusive, anti-oppressive and empowering approach to complex situations.
- Sculpts highlight the potential for professional perceptions to mirror the position of the individuals on which they are focussed.

- Sculpts have the capacity to make explicit the assumptions and discourses that delineate professional roles and responsibilities.
- Sculpts bring alive the affective dimensions of family and professional dynamics, which in turn help make sense of the behaviours of individuals.

Reflective Activity

Think of family with whom you are currently working and where you feel 'stuck'.

- How might you engage the family in participating in a sculpt?
- How would you describe what sculpting involves?
- What resistance might you encounter?
- How would you respond to it?
- What might be the benefits of doing a sculpt?

Reflective conversations

Another reflective approach that draws on systemic thinking and is used with families is the reflective conversation. The basic premise of reflective conversations is that they create an opportunity for families to listen to professionals 'wondering' or 'hypothesising' about the current difficulties being encountered in a family. 'Curiousity', a term coined by Cecchin (1987), a systemic therapist, encapsulates what is happening in reflective conversations. Practitioners explore in front of the family what has caught their attention, what assumptions they have noticed they (or others) have been holding, which discourses seem to be most apparent, what has been asked and answered and what remains unaddressed. Adopting a position of curiosity allows practitioners to retain a 'not knowing' stance, open to different explanations and possible outcomes. As such, it prevents practitioners taking on positions of expertise, reaching premature conclusions/decisions and allowing the family to be experts on their own lives. One of the strengths of reflective conversations is their capacity to make the dynamics between the professionals and the family members transparent and empowering. Reimers (1995, cited in Martyn, 2000) refers to social workers as needing to be 'explorers' as opposed to experts when working with children and families, and reflective conversations encourage the development of this professional identity.

Reflective conversations can happen in a variety of ways. In reflective teams two workers in the room relate directly with the family and two workers act as observers either in the room as non-participant observers or behind a one-way screen. In the course of the meeting the two direct workers will invite the two observers to hold a reflective conversation in front of the family. Reflective conversations are governed by several guiding principles which include:

- Engage in conversation rather than monologues.
- Be aware of the negative impact of attributing blame for behaviours.

- Introduce some difference in perspective but not too much difference.
- Reflect in a speculative and curious manner, e.g. 'I wonder what would happen if...', or 'I was struck by how. ...'
- Keep the conversations brief and restrict them to a few ideas.
- Use accessible, 'everyday' language and the terminology of the people who are engaged in the session.

Following the reflective exchange the family are invited by the direct workers to reflect on the comments, observations and musings of the observers. One of the main benefits of a reflective team is the differing perspectives that arise from the observers who are not engaged directly with the content of the session. In an observational role practitioners are more able to comment on the processes and family dynamics, which can be difficult to recognise and comment on when responsible for conducting the interview. A modification on the reflective team that requires fewer workers is for two practitioners to co-work with a family. Both practitioners are in the room with the family. One practitioner takes the lead role and engages with the family, whilst the other practitioner adopts a more observational stance. In the course of the session the two workers conduct a reflective conversation with each other, again in front of the family commenting on the process of the session and issues that have made them curious. In situations where practitioners are working individually with a family it is still possible for a reflective conversation to be held. In these instances the practitioners can invite a member of the family to join with them to consider what has gone on. This can be particularly empowering for family members who feel marginalised or scapegoated in the family and can generate new and creative family dynamics and responses.

Case example

Undertaking work with families where sexual abuse has taken place challenges the beliefs and values of individuals located in the family and professional groups concerned. Utilising reflective conversations is one way of making these often privately held beliefs and values explicit.

A mother, Carol, and step-father, Bob, with their 15-year-old daughter, Natalie, attended sessions at a family centre. The purpose of the sessions was to explore with the family how safe it was for the step-father to be reintegrated into the family home. Bob had recently been released from prison having served a sentence for sexually abusing a 7-year-old child several years previously. In the course of the child protection assessment process, Social Services had enforced strict contracts on the family, which detailed how the family could relate to each other and maintain contact. At the point of referral to the family centre, the child protection team was requesting an assessment of how safe it was for Bob to move back in with Carol and Natalie. During the course of the Family Centre meetings a reflective team worked with the family. Two team members conducted reflective conversations in front of the family. In the course of one of these conversations a practitioner commented on how the child protection team's response to the risk and uncertainty inherent in this family's circumstances was to try to eliminate all risk by prescribing how the family behaved and imposing increasingly rigorous and restrictive contracts on them. From this practitioner's perspective the assessment process had not invited the family to voice their perspectives and to suggest how they might protect Natalie. In addition the reflecting team commented that the requirement for Bob to only have contact with Carol and Natalie during daytime hours suggested that sexual abuse was understood to only happen at night. By reflecting on this assumption and wondering how else Natalie might be protected the family were able to respond with their own ideas and to compile a written agreement with the Family Centre that invited the family to take responsibility for protecting Natalie, rather than having requirements imposed on them. The reflective conversation illustrated how dealing with cases involving sexual abuse can distort professional thinking and generate emotionally charged, defensive and risk-averse responses.

The work of the reflective team, in this instance, was characterised by the ability of the practitioners to address issues at both a content and process level, with the emotional reactions to sexual abuse being recognised as having a potentially powerful and distorting impact on effective professional practice. As a consequence there was greater scope for doubt and uncertainty to be voiced, alongside an increase in the scope for risk-taking and creative practice. Within the sessions the workers spent time in detailed conversation with the family, exploring their experiences of social work intervention, their thoughts and feelings about what had happened and their fears and fantasies for the family's future. By 'wondering out loud' and acknowledging that eliminating risk was not possible but managing it was, the Family Centre practitioners were able to work in partnership with the family and construct a realistic assessment and action plan. The outcome of this dialogically based, reflective approach was an intervention which appeared to empower the family to identify their own safeguards rather than having them defined and imposed by social services. Reflective conversations are inclusive and respectful and ensure that all parties contribute to further planning and interventions. If the diverse perspectives held by different individuals involved in a situation are not explored the scope for authentic partnership work and effective solutions is significantly reduced.

Learning points

- There are multiple perspectives on all situations.
- Attending to process issues is as important as addressing the content.
- A position of curiosity embraces difference and diversity and enhances the likelihood of arriving at solutions suited to the specific individuals/circumstances.
- Reflective conversations are potentially empowering and anti-oppressive.

Individual work with children and young people

Debates, definitions and therapeutic interventions

In light of the Climbié inquiry, time spent individually with a child has become top priority for all social work practitioners, whether they are located in assessment teams or in longer term teams involved with children who are looked after (Laming Inquiry social care recommendations 26 and 35). At the same time the increasing fragmentation of children's services and the distinctions drawn between those practitioners who commission and purchase services for children and families and those who provide the services has created confusion and tension about what spending time with a child on their own is supposed to achieve and what individual work with children is comprised of. There is considerable uncertainty amongst 'purchasing practitioners', usually based in Local Authority contexts, as to the extent to which their remit allows for work with individual children. Most social workers located in statutory assessment and longer-term child care teams do not consider they have the time or the expertise to undertake individual work. From this perspective individual work with a child/young person is regarded as the exclusive domain of therapeutic experts, such as child psychotherapists or clinical psychologists. As a result there is a misconception of individual work with children only being done in therapeutic contexts such as Child Guidance Clinics and CAMHS teams or occasionally in preventative/specialist settings such as Sure Start and voluntary sector projects. The alternative, and equally misguided, perception of individual work, is that it is a straightforward task, usually undertaken to comply with organisational requirements such as the 'looked after children' regulations. From this perspective individual work is a bureaucratic and administrative exercise, requiring little skill or professional expertise. It is important to challenge these misconceptions.

Part of the confusion arises from established terminology. 'Direct work', is the term that has been most commonly used to describe discrete pieces of work with a specific focus, usually undertaken by social work practitioners in longer-term child care teams with individual children. There is, however, a longstanding debate about what exactly 'direct work' with children/young people is and is not. A significant element of this debate is the disputed understanding of the terms therapy and therapeutic. One definition of therapy is 'to look after, to attend to, to heal'. In its broadest sense, all social work with children is about attending to their needs and is, by definition, therapeutic. Regardless of whether the work undertaken is ostensibly 'less therapeutic' such as one-off assessment visits, statutory review visits or child protection investigations or 'more therapeutic', such as planned sessions with a particular aim of producing, for example, a life story book for a child, all social work engagement with children has a therapeutic component. Car journeys with children are frequently cited by practitioners as important opportunities for therapeutic encounters and should not be dismissed as of little significance. Residential social workers are all too familiar with small incidents and encounters provoking seemingly disproportionate responses from a child, responses that in the child's mind 'make sense'. How practitioners respond to these daily occurrences and oppurtunities is crucial to a child's well-being (Ward, 2008). From a therapeutic perspective nothing is meaningless, all behaviours are purposeful and require thoughtful responses. Such responses are therapeutic in nature.

In addressing these debates and dilemmas, changes in terminology might go some way to correcting the prevailing confusion. Direct work and therapy, often used mutually exclusively, can be replaced with the term 'focussed therapeutic work with children and young people' as a more accurate title for the broad range of work with children and young people that social workers engage in. Incorporating the word 'focussed' into the description of work being undertaken distinguishes the focused therapeutic work of social workers from the longer term, often less directive therapeutic work undertaken by other professionals such as psychotherapists, clinical psychologists and play therapists. Ensuring the word therapeutic is included in the description of work done by social worker practitioners ensures it does not get diminished and devalued to the level of a purely administrative exercise that supports procedurally driven child care practices. Charles' (2004) chapter titled 'Creativity and Constraint in Child Welfare', in a book entitled *Social Work Ideals and Practice Realities* captures (along with the books title) the essence of this tension. Charles' (2004:179) recognises

the gap between the organisational realities of proceduralisation and standardisation and the practice ideals of working creatively with children young people.

In the current climate, effectiveness, efficiency and economy are prioritised, relationships are undervalued and emotions are denied (Charles, 2004). Relationship-based and reflective practices, i.e. therapeutic practices, within procedural frameworks, are crucial for effecting positive change in children, young people and their caring networks.

So what do practitioners need to know to and what skills do they need to have to undertake focussed therapeutic work with children and young people?

Theoretical underpinnings

One of the main foundations on which individual social work with children is built is psychoanalytic theory. Psychoanalytically informed perspectives place considerable importance on the influence of early experiences on later development. Sigmund and Anna Freud, Melanie Klein and Donald Winnicott are important contributors to psychoanalytic ideas and thinking (Hunter, 2001; Trowell, 1995). There are three key features of psychoanalytic theoretical perspectives that are widely recognised to be important:

- Past experiences affect current attitudes and behaviour.
- Behaviours are not always conscious and can be influenced by unconscious experiences.
- Relationships are central to development. The relationship between a child/young person and practitioner can be influenced and affected by experiences of other, unconnected experiences and relationships that are not always consciously recognised.

Some of the key psychoanalytic concepts that social workers need to have a basic understanding of are:

- Transference and counter-transference
- Projection and introjection
- Defence mechanisms – denial, repression, regression, sublimation, splitting

Bower (2005) and Trowell (1995) provide concise and accessible introductions to these concepts.

In contrast to child psychotherapists and play therapists, who focus in their work exclusively on the child's inner world, social workers are required to make connections with the child's social context and what this means to them internally. Psychoanalytic perspectives are helpful theoretical tools for understanding the complex dynamics that can arise in individual work with children. As a theoretical framework informing psychodynamic social work practices, psychoanalysis has fallen out of favour in recent decades, yet as Stevenson (2005:ix) acknowledges, at the same time, it is also 'part and parcel of our collective understanding of behaviours'. Most people accept the existence of dreams, a manifestation of unconscious processes and the term 'Freudian slip' is common parlance. Some key psychodynamic concepts are important and discussed further below. It is imperative, however, that social workers in drawing on psychodynamic concepts recognise the limits of their expertise and are alert to the difficulties and shortcomings of psychoanalytic ideas (Stevenson, 2005). Social workers are not qualified to interpret the unconscious material that children bring to individual sessions but it is not possible when working with a child to stop unconscious processes operating. Psychoanalytic thinking does not have a monopoly on understanding work with children and young people but its ideas can be informative and need to be understood for effective practice. The demanding nature of working with children and young people and the complexity of psychodynamic thinking heighten the importance of practitioners having appropriate reflective spaces where they can think about their practice experiences.

Reflective skills for focussed therapeutic work

Social work practitioners can be engaged with a child or young person for a wide range of reasons. The list below is not definitive but represents a compilation of the main reasons for working therapeutically with children and young people as identified by Carroll (1998) and Brandon *et al.* (2000):

- To make sense of confusing events in the past, understand and come to terms with feelings about those who may have abused them and to prepare for life in a new family
- To enable the child to understand and leave behind the emotional baggage associated with destructive early life experiences
- To 'make up for' some early lost experiences, especially missed opportunities to play
- To enable child to experience the full range of emotions, pleasurable as well as painful
- To enable child to modify anti-social behaviour
- To improve child's self-esteem
- To enable child to express their view

There is a wide range of tools and techniques available to practitioners working individually with children and young people (Oaklander, 1978). To address any of the issues identified above or combinations of them requires practitioners to be familiar with child-centred approaches but these are not sufficient in themselves. Understanding how to use a particular tool in an effective and reflective way requires considerable self-awareness and reflective capability.

Focussed therapeutic techniques

Practitioners will be familiar with exercises for working with children and young people such as ecomaps, lifemaps and genograms. It is rare, however, for practitioners to have had the experience of being a recipient of these exercises. By direct and personal experience of an exercise such as a life map, practitioners gain an insight into the powerful nature of what can appear to be quite straightforward techniques for working directly with children. As part of their reflective learning and development pairs of practitioners (taking up positions as recipient and/or facilitator) can complete any of the exercises they use with children.

Reflective Activity

Withacolleaguedecideonatherapeuticexercisetoundertake,e.g.anecomaporlifemap.Takeit inturnstobetheexercisefacilitatorandrecipient.Oncompletionoftheexerciseaskyourselves, and discuss together, the following questions:

- HowdidIfeelaboutcompletingthisexercise(asrecipientorfacilitator)–before,duringand after?
- Whatdolobserveaboutmyresponsesandbehaviours(asrecipientorfacilitator)duringthe exercise?
- What influences how I behave?
- What have I discovered?
- What has surprised me?

In introducing the lifemap and ecomap exercises to practitioners on post-qualification courses it is possible to observe how psychoanalytic ideas can help make sense of what occurs. The process of transference can operate, for example, with the recipient having expectations of how to behave in response to the facilitator that are rooted in earlier personal or professional experiences that they may or may not be conscious of. Some practitioners when being the recipient of the exercise can resort to defensive behaviours to prevent having to explore aspects of their experiences that are too difficult to face. On one occasion a pair giggled excessively during the exercise but on reflection with the wider group after wards they were able to recognise their behaviour as an avoidance of painful issues. Three consistent responses have arisen when discussing the task on its completion with practitioners:

- Despite being familiar with the exercises, recipients were surprised at the powerful and potentially intrusive nature of the exercise and their feeling that the facilitator was not always sufficiently sensitive to their feeling of vulnerability/self-exposure or to their non-verbal cues.
- The centrality of the relationship with the facilitator – recipients were aware of monitoring what they did/did not say depending on how they related to the facilitator.
- The sensitive way in which power dynamics need to be handled – often the exercise was prescribed by the facilitator, for example by automatically holding the pen and taking charge of drawing the lifemap/ecomap.

The use of specific therapeutic tools has not been without criticism. Simmonds (1988), an advocate for individual work with children and young people, recognised the potentially dangerous situation, given the paucity of literature and guidance about therapeutic approaches which were relevant and appropriate for social workers, coinciding with an increasingly available and easily assimilated range of techniques. He warned that these techniques had:

> to be tempered with the realisation of the difficulties for both worker and child in developing a close and significant relationship. The pressure on social workers to stay within the theoretical limits of their role is at odds with

the reality of children and families in trouble, presenting complex issues that do not easily succumb to rational discussion or understanding.

(Simmonds, 1988:19)

By experiencing the exercises personally practitioners can begin to understand the therapeutic potential of these approaches and become aware of the skill and sensitivity that is required to realise this potential. One practitioner commented on this experience in her assignment. Relating the experience to work she had undertaken with a teenage girl, Nina, the practitioner wrote:

During the experiential process of action learning sets I felt empathy for Nina… Whilst applying systemic techniques and having my own family's 'limitations' publicly discussed I realised how as social workers we often implement therapeutic techniques knowing that dysfunction will be exposed – yet without consideration for how this may leave young people feeling. I realised that when we apply direct working strategies we are often so focussed on our agenda that we neglect to consider the feelings of inadequacy and guilt that young people may be left with. We may come away feeling we have achieved what we intended – yet without realising that the young person may not leave with a similar sense of achievement.

(PQ candidate)

Gaining a personal insight into the impact of these techniques is an important way of developing a more relationship-based and reflective position, which is crucial to effectiveness:

Knowledge of others cannot be acquired without knowledge of oneself. Knowledge of others cannot be a substitute for knowledge of oneself. Knowledge of oneself cannot be acquired without a relationship with others.

(Simmonds, 1998:96)

This heightened awareness of self and of the complexity and challenges of working with children and young people reinforces the need for sound theoretical frameworks and appropriate support mechanisms for practitioners.

Learning points

- Therapeutic exercises need to be individualised for each child/young person and implemented in a reflective manner.
- The power of seemingly straightforward techniques must not be underestimated.
- Psychodynamic theoretical frameworks help to 'make sense' of the relational complexities of focussed therapeutic work.
- The process and dynamics of the exercise and encounter is as important as its content.
- All individual work requires adequate support for the practitioner to cope with the demanding nature of the work and to ensure its potential is realised.
- Individual exercises and techniques can be adapted to use with families.

Affective and reflective evaluation tools

One of the most difficult aspects of working with a child or young person is working out what is to be achieved and when and how this will be realised and recognised. The current bureaucratic and outcome driven climate of social work means evaluating work is a familiar process. Practitioners might be asked to evaluate their own practice as part of their continuing professional development or service users can be requested to comment on experiences of the intervention received. Both usually involve completing a form. As with all procedural tools evaluation forms have their uses but practitioners can as usefully develop an affective and reflective means of evaluating their practice. Affective evaluations are undertaken at the commencement and on conclusion of the overall piece of work prior to and before and after individual sessions with the child/young person. Practitioners are encouraged to identify at the outset:

- Their aims/objectives for the session/whole piece of work
- Issues from their own biography that might impact on the work to be undertaken
- Their feelings about the session/whole piece of work prior to it and after it

On concluding a session or piece of work practitioners are encouraged to ask themselves:

- What am I feeling now at the end of the session/work?
- Can I identify what has contributed to these feelings?
- What has been most effective/least effective? Can I identify why?
- What should happen next?

It is all too easy to become blinkered and resort to repetitive but unhelpful strategies for achieving an outcome that is imposed from the outside as opposed to one identified by the child/young person and the practitioner. On one occasion I had arranged to undertake life story work with Paul, a young boy of 7. The imperative for this work came from the Adoption and Fostering Panel who were needing to make decisions about his long-term future and expected evidence of work undertaken with him. Every time I arrived to undertake the work the boy proved difficult to engage and by the end of the six sessions I had planned I had little to show for my input other than two pages in a file. I had repeatedly tried to engage Paul on each visit altering my approach but keeping focussed on the life story book work. It was only as I took the time to evaluate the sessions and to reflect on them individually and in supervision that it became apparent that Paul was simply not ready to think about his past circumstances. A comment to Paul that acknowledged this understanding may well have unlocked far more than I had been able to. Unfortunately my misguided preoccupation was with the expectations of the Panel and my fear of being considered incompetent because of my lack of progress with life story work. An affective and reflective evaluation of this experience may well have enabled me to realise sooner what was happening and to either adopt a different approach or at the very least to present this understanding to the Panel. With an honest and informed account of the work, albeit incomplete in this case in the eyes of the Panel, more accurate decisions and plans can be reached.

The purpose of affective evaluations is to encourage practitioners to recognise the valuable information that their feelings can offer them. Rarely does work with children and young people, however well prepared, go to plan. Practitioners have to be spontaneous and creative. Treating feelings as facts balances out the tendency, particularly associated with evidence-based practice agendas, to privilege hard knowledge, such as research, a theoretical framework or specific well-recognised therapeutic techniques, at the expense of the softer, more personal sources of knowledge. An additional spin-off of undertaking evaluations of this type is the attention practitioners give to the process of the sessions/piece of work as much as their content. This shift in emphasis towards process helps to redefine narrowly conceived understandings of outcomes. It values the child-practitioner relationship and considers 'soft' evidence and outcomes', for example, about the quality of the relationship, to be as important as 'hard' evidence and outcomes, for example, a child having a clearer understanding of their circumstances.

A further benefit of affective evaluative procedures concerns their compatibility with reflective practice. To develop their reflective capabilities, practitioners need to be able to integrate intellectual rigour with emotional awareness. The two need to go hand in hand and tools such as affective evaluation facilitate this inter-dependence. As one practitioner put it in her assignment:

> One particular learning point that struck me from systems thinking was that I, as the social worker, 'am part and parcel of the child's real world' (Kanter, 2005:171) and that I cannot therefore be completely detached from it. This realisation has better equipped me to consider how can therefore use this position effectively whilst remaining as objective as I can.

> (PQ candidate)

Through affective evaluation processes, recognition of affective responses can be made sense of with the help of psychodynamic theoretical concepts and processes such as transference, projection or defensive behaviours.

Learning points

- It is important to keep objectives and outcomes of focussed therapeutic work realistic, which can often mean they are very small.
- Objectives and outcomes, in the first instance, must be meaningful to the child/young person rather than the professional system.
- The pace of the work is all important and must be set by the child/young person circumstances.

Conclusion

To hold a child in mind practitioners need to hold themselves in mind too. In doing so practitioners are able to make every encounter with a child or young people, however, small or fleeting, therapeutic and even when mistakes are made they can be positively connoted as Martyn (2000:8) recognises:

> *... becoming a professional worker does not obliterate human frailty. It remains a vital professional responsibility to address boundary issues (personal/professional) in order to be available to users, but there are some situations*

where users may gain something from our frailties as well as our strengths. The role of supervision is crucial in order for an appropriate boundary to be discerned, reviewed and maintained.

It is important that the reflective skills explored in this chapter become familiar for practitioners engaging with children and their caring networks. With these skills 'under their belt' practitioners can engage with service users in a range of ways, confident that their interventions will be in the best interests of the people with whom they are working and have the greatest potential possible for promoting positive change.

Chapter summary

- Working with children, young people, their families, carers and professional networks is a complex and challenging area of practice that requires practitioners to sensitively manage the tension between the needs of the child/young people and their wider networks.
- Working with families and professional systems is assisted by the use of multi-faceted approaches such as sculpting and reflective conversations.
- Individual work with children/young people requires practitioners to develop competence with using approaches for focussed therapeutic work in a reflective manner.
- Developing a repertoire of reflective skills and techniques ensures work with individual and their wider systems remains sensitive to their uniqueness.

Reflective questions

What is your biggest concern about engaging with a child/young person? What would help you address this concern?

What is your understanding of the term 'therapeutic' and how does it influence the sort of work you undertake?

When working therapeutically with a child what informs what you do? What sources of knowledge do you find you least draw upon and how could you redress the balance?

How might you adapt approaches for working with individuals to work with families/wider networks?

Notes

1. The sculpt example used in this chapter was first published in an article in Groupwork under the title 'Nothing New under the Sun: Using Sculpts in Post-qualification Child Care Social Work Groups', Groupwork, 16, 2.
2. With grateful thanks to Rachael Williams and Hazel Chapman (PQ candidates) for permission to include extracts from their PQ assignments.

Chapter 10

Innovatory and regulatory practice in contemporary childcare social work

Teri Rogers

Chapter learning aims

- To identify and understand the impact on childcare practice of changes in the processes of accountability, regulation and management
- To develop a critically reflective understanding of assessment and risk frameworks to ensure maximum benefits for children and young people
- To identify and consider creative and innovatory practice with children and young people

Introduction

Professional practice involves working within the parameters of the legal and policy context, but not seeking to follow guidelines and established practice mechanistically or unthinkingly.

(Thompson, 2002:121)

This chapter seeks to explore how the recent changes in the organisation and delivery of services have impacted upon childcare practice and the ability of practitioners to be innovative and creative. Changes in childcare social work practice have occurred against the broader backdrop of the risk society and consequently most of the changes that have taken place have involved increased regulation and monitoring of the practice task both professionally and individually (Jones, 2001). Alongside this there is increasing scrutiny from both inside and outside of the practice environment. There has been major debate regarding the delivery of effective childcare services for over 20 years, from the development of markets and purchaser–provider splits introduced by the Conservatives in the 1980s to New Labour's modernising agenda in the late 1990s. A recurrent theme arising from inspections and child death inquiries is that social work practice needs to change (Reder and Duncan, 2004). Most recently the inquiry into the death of Victoria Climbié (DoH, 2003) resulted in substantial legislative and policy changes, embodied in the Children Act 2004 and the Every Child Matters agenda.

The challenge for childcare social workers is how to maintain creativity and innovation in a climate of increasing risk awareness, regulation, resource restrictions and limited staff numbers. The recruitment and retention difficulties within the social work profession have been evident for some time and remain a particular challenge within the field of childcare social work. The combination of highly stressed workers operating within resource constraints, torn between achieving targets set by the organisation and meeting the needs of the child, does not create the optimum environment for innovation and creativity. It is easy at times like these to use the protection offered by regulation and procedure but, as the above quote suggests, whilst working within such parameters, they should be recognised as only one of several important components necessary for effective practice.

The chapter begins by outlining the socio-political context of contemporary childcare social work and in particular the emergence of the 'risk society'. The impact of risk on childcare assessment practice and the interaction between risks and need, both in terms of how they are quantified and regulated, are explored, as are the Government agendas shaping social work practice. The tensions embedded in these agendas and their relationship to the concept of risk are the focus of the middle section of the chapter, with particular attention paid to the role of regulation and accountability, managerialism, surveillance and supervision and the nature of evidence in practice. In the concluding section of the chapter the challenges and opportunities for innovative and creative practice are discussed, along with an example of how this can be achieved.

The socio-political context of practice

The relationship between childcare practice and the context in which it operates is a symbiotic one, they are interdependent upon each other and shaped by others' existence. It is not possible to separate practice from the context in which it occurs. Over the past twenty years that context has been subject to considerable legislative, policy and regulatory changes and has seen a shift in traditional views of social work practice that has led to a questioning of its very nature as a profession. One of the most influential forces shaping contemporary childcare social work practice is the concept of risk.

The contested nature of risk and the risk society

In recent years risk has become a major theme in public policy and it is a complex and multifaceted concept (see Chapter 7 and Beck, 1992). Risk pervades society in general, and contemporary social work practice in particular, being most evident in the extent to which practice is risk tolerant or risk averse. Jaeger *et al.* (2001:9) argue that risk, as we know it, is 'wholly a child of the late twentieth century'. Hood *et al.* (2001) challenge the notion of a risk society arguing that it is not dramatic changes in the scale or nature of contemporary risk but well-known policy influences such as public opinion and market forces that influence risk management. Alaszewski and Manthorpe (1998) make a helpful distinction as to how organisations manage risk. Bureaucratic organisations tend to be staff-centred rather than user-centred and in these contexts the social worker is likely to be seen as the 'expert' with the focus of activity being risk averse aimed at anticipating and preventing risk. In contrast service user-centred agencies are more flexible and risk tolerant, tending to delegate decision-making and valuing independent judgement. They are more likely to develop rapid responses than to spend energy trying to predict and prevent specific risks.

An additional dimension to the risk society is that, in the face of such risks at global and local levels, individuals also have more options and autonomy to manage their life course than ever before and must develop and take responsibility for this, a perspective that links to some of the ideas associated with the 'New Labour' concept of responsibility, discussed below.

Making sense of and managing risk in childcare social work

Within children and families practice risk is not a discrete legal concept but is enshrined in the Children Act 1989 in terms of significant harm. The term 'significant harm' brings into place many variables, such as age and condition of the individual, together with social norms and legal decisions and appeals. As a consequence the context of the definition of 'significant harm' is constantly changing, leaving practitioners working in situations of uncertainty.

In response to conditions of uncertainty, increased proceduralisation can be seen as a 'quest for certainty' and Kemshall and Pritchard (1996) argue that increasing regulation is an attempt to eliminate risk, forcing practitioners into practice that is dominated by risk management. Quality is measured against prioritising, monitoring and reducing risk and the pre-occupation with risk has changed the way workers think about and approach it (Parton, 1998). These changes in professional perspective are set against a backdrop of public (and inter-professional) distrust in social workers 'claimed expertise', generated by the recurrence of high profile child abuse inquiries, of which Victoria Climbié (DoH, 2003) is the most recent.

Throughout the 1990s risk tended to focus upon pathologising individual behaviour and practice tended to focus on the simple question 'was this child abused or not?' Wider social economic factors contributing to risk tended to be ignored. Public policy was focussed on the forensic rather than predictive use of risk by means of investigation (Kemshall, 2002). Research in this period (Thoburn, et al., 1995), however, concluded that not only was this approach to risk ineffective but at times it was oppressive, with the number of child protection investigations taking place outnumbering those requiring intervention by 80%. There was a growing consensus that risk was a yardstick to manage scarce resources and social workers were accountable for managing those risks.

In addition the growing 'blame culture', associated with the 'damned if you do and damned if you don't' philosophy in professional practice (Steele, 1998), contributed to the creation of professional contexts in which individual accountability became a disincentive to risk-taking. For Gurney (2000) the responsibility for risk-taking and allocation of blame when things go wrong varies according to how far risk is seen as a consequence of social structures and conditions or is attributed to individual behaviour or shortcomings. When the individualistic perspective dominates the belief systems of professionals, they are more inclined to engage in risk-averse activities for fear of reprisals.

Recognition of the escalation of risk-averse childcare social work practice in the 1990s culminated in the 'refocusing debate' (DoH, 1995), which involved a conscious shift in professional perspective from a risk-driven approach to one prioritising prevention, family support services and the consideration of risk within a continuum of the child's level of need. The earlier preoccupation with whether or not abuse had occurred was replaced by broader-based concern for the needs of the child, including those for protection. The Framework for Assessment (DoH, 2000) was the major tool used to achieve this purpose, with the introduction of a holistic framework for assessing children's needs which moved away from individual pathology to focus on the child within an environmental context and upon strengths rather than weaknesses. The aim was for risk to be seen as a continuum between control and legal authority at one end and empowerment at the other, with risk management located somewhere between the two ends of this continuum (Gurney, 2000).

Despite its strengths the Framework for Assessment has not been without its critics, particularly because of the wider emphasis on regulation and audit (discussed below), as it did not use any specific tool for risk management and relied solely on professional judgement for analysis and decision-making. It is possible to conclude that risk was avoided within the design of this Assessment Framework. Cooper (2004), however, refutes this and argues that there is a complex risk management structure embedded within the Framework but suggests that risk is too complicated to quantify and to understand the nature of risk requires risk relations to be measured across and between each category of the domains.

Parton (1998) also recognised the challenges to contemporary childcare social work of the risk-ridden culture. According to Parton childcare policy is based on the dual but conflicting principles of partnership with families/family support and protection of children/prevention of significant harm. Assessing risk has similar conflicts in terms of the need to ascertain what is calculable and predictable and accepting what is incalculable and coping with uncertainty. Stalker (2003:223) neatly encapsulates this professional challenge recognising that:

> Notions of ambiguity, uncertainty and complexity lie at the heart of social work and working with, rather than against this, will produce more creative and innovative responses.

Cooper (2004) discusses how the management of risk appears to have developed what he terms 'a certainty strategy'. The 'certainty strategy' is based on what Cooper considers to be a more realistic response to the inevitability of risk in professional practice. Rather than trying to create certainty where it does not exist, the certainty strategy is based on the belief that if risk is identified there is a 99% certainty it will reoccur, unless proven otherwise. In line with Cooper's ideas, Parton (1998) advocates that practitioners should develop mutually trusting and respectful relationships with service users, make fine judgements about risk and dare to work creatively and innovatively, moving towards a more positive framework for risk-taking behaviour, with the potential to empower through risk being understood as a normal part of everyday life.

Risk management increasingly requires practitioners to follow procedures and guidelines. The introduction of a new information sharing system, the Common Assessment Framework (CAF), is highlighting, however, that this professional requirement is not entirely straightforward or easily achieved. The overall aim of the CAF is to try to manage risk through improved systems of information sharing and more structured and effective referrals between agencies. Failures in communication was one of the most pressing issues of the Laming Inquiry and for most of the inquiries into childcare tragedies held in the last 30 years.

The creation of national database to be known as the Information Sharing Index (ISI) together with the CAF are the two major stands being put into operation practically to try and address issues of communication. The ISI should be fully operational by March 2008 and will record the names of the agencies, professionals and the universal and targeted services received for every child in England, together with demographic and family information. Guidance on issues relating to consent, eligibility and access to the database is currently being developed. The basic principle underlying the ISI of early sharing of information between and across agencies is a sound one and strongly aligned with the underlying ethos of early intervention and prevention, however, there are a number of potential problems in the practical application of the database that may undermine its effectiveness in identifying children in need and those in need of protection:

- The accuracy of the information stored upon the system is one factor. There is massive potential for human error in inputting data and despite the infrastructure being put in place the information will only be as good as that supplied. The government does not have a good track record in this area. In the case of the Child Support Agency, Munro (2005) found an 86% error rate on the police national computer. Costs could become prohibitive and estimates are that the cost of maintaining the systems once up and running could be in the region of £41 million annually (see www.everychildmatters.gov.uk).

- The question has to be asked whether the database will reach the most vulnerable children such as refugees, those privately fostered and itinerant families. Would, for example, Victoria Climbié have made it onto such a database, entering the country as she did with nothing known of her previous life?

- How will families view such a database given current views that intervention is often heavy handed, punitive and crisis-driven? The ideal would be information is shared about vulnerable children in an effective, non-stigmatising and non-crisis focussed climate; however, this has to be viewed alongside what Precey (2006:19) describes as:

...an employment environment in which family social workers are becoming an increasingly disappearing breed amid tectonic shifts in the organisations of social welfare provision and funding that exhorts single agencies to emerge from their 'silos' and reorganise into multi-agency delivery systems.

- One of the intentions of the CAF is to locate the provision of services to children in need in non-social work agencies at an earlier stage without the stigmatisation so often associated with social work intervention. The CAF has been welcomed as a way of giving more control to other agencies such as health and education, of lessening the need to rely on social work services and of managing the disputes regarding eligibility criteria and thresholds for intervention that are so often a source of frustrations between agencies. The CAF, however, cannot completely eradicate this debate, as inevitably differences in perception about what constitutes the need for protection or disagreement regarding the interpretation of risk will continue. The CAF relies on assessors having a grasp of risk indicators to know when to bring a situation to the attention of social workers. Much effort has been directed in this area such as the guidelines *What to do if you are worried a child is being abused* (DoH, 2003). It is the initial recognition of those risk factors that is the biggest challenge if the

CAF is going to be effective in early identification of risk. Boody, Wigfull and Simon (2007) in their evaluation of one of the twelve CAF trailblazing sites found that such early intervention is a challenge to the well-known statutory role of children and families workers and felt this role at times conflicts with new community-based type worker proposed within Every Child Matters, but social workers played an invaluable role in providing support and advice to other professionals in the crucial elements of risk identification. They firmly advocate a new community role for social work in implementing universal services and practice developments such as family centres and extended schools.

A central source of concern arising from the preoccupation with risk and proceduralisation of practice, of which the CAF is one example, is its impact on professional judgement. To date, there is limited evidence about the relationship between procedures and professional judgments (Macdonald and Macdonald, 1999), nor about how managers can promote good judgement within or perhaps in spite of the regulatory framework (Parsloe, 1999). Dalgleish (2004) uses signal detection theory to try and identify impacts upon decision-making and risk. He concludes by supporting Rossi, Shuermann and Budde's (1996) idea of the 'Common Scale Varying Threshold Hypothesis'. This posits that practitioners use similar information and quantify risk in the same way but how they rate risk (high, medium or low) and to what extent they are prepared to manage that risk, is not so much linked with the case factors identified but with the value the individual practitioner places upon intervention in the family and their practice environment. The impact of getting it wrong, an individualised blame culture, and procedural rigidity were all factors that appeared to lead to risk-aversive and defensive-type practices.

Learning points

- Risk is a complex concept firmly fixed within the norms and culture of the society.
- Increased regulation and procedures have aimed to measure risk in terms of predictability and 'certainty' whereas social work operates in a climate of ambiguity and uncertainty.
- Risk operates along a continuum from social control to empowerment; where the individual practitioner positions themselves is a combination of their core values and operational environment.

Reflective Activity

Think about a recent case where you have had to quantify risk. In making your analysis how much did the following factors impact on your decision:

- Your own values
- The views of your peers
- The views of your manager

- The culture of your organisation
- Procedural requirements
- Service user assessments of risk
- The need to 'get it right'

Try ranking them from 1 to 5, with 5 being the most influential factor.

- What are the main factors influencing you in managing risk?
- Taking these into account, where would you place yourself on this continuum and are you satisfied with this position?

Avoids risk .... Prepared to take risks

Alongside, and connected to, the growing influence of risk on social work practice, other significant social, economic and political forces, namely the modernisation agenda and the reconfiguration of the role of the professional, have been shaping how practice is understood and operationalised.

Modernising social work agendas

Up until the 1980s childcare social workers were providers of welfare services. With the introduction of markets under the Conservative government, social services became responsible for commissioning services and contracts, and service level agreements and case management were introduced as the core characteristics of the new 'mixed economy of welfare'. This change in the organisation and delivery of services involved a shift towards increasing regulation and accountability and a burgeoning role for managers, giving them control over budgets and the quality of the services they delivered. With the election in 1997 of a Labour Government these trends towards the 'marketisation of welfare' continued under the guise of New Labour and its 'modernising agenda', with continuing implications for both the social work profession and social work practice (Hendrick, 2003; Jordan and Jordan, 2000).

Another central theme of the government-driven modernising agenda, interestingly developed by both Conservative and Labour Governments, was the idea of rights and responsibilities, as evidenced, for example, in the Children Act 1989, which shifted its focus away from parental rights to parental responsibilities. More recently the Children Act 2004 has reiterated the Laming Report (DoH, 2003) that safeguarding children is everyone's responsibility. This stance has been termed 'tough love' (Jordan, 2004) – the notion of support being available but countered by compulsory action if the stakeholder does not take up the services on offer or uphold those responsibilities. This approach is clearly visible within the youth offending arena where supportive services to parents and interventions with young people are backed up by more coercive measures such as Anti-Social Behaviour Orders (ASBOs) and Parenting Orders. Such policies provide for a process of renegotiation regarding individual responsibilities and the state, with the social worker positioned as the conduit, delivering services to the most vulnerable, with clear expectations that along with independence and choice also comes responsibility (Parton, 2005).

One serious consequence of this new approach is a greater mistrust on the part of other professionals about the desirability of working with or being seen to be working with those whose primary tasks appear to be reactive i.e. removing children from their families or surveillance of those families (Tunstill *et al.*, 2005). This situation is exacerbated by the number of high profile child deaths and fears amongst professionals of the all-pervasive 'blame culture' that permeates child welfare. When placed in this context it becomes clear why developing effective inter-professional working relationships is so challenging (see Chapter 11).

Within the modernising agenda it is possible to identify three implicit strands that link to childcare social work:

- Reduction of social deprivation through the provision of universal services
- Reform of the tax system – child-related benefits such as working tax credits, employment opportunities for lone parents/parents under auspices of the National Childcare Strategy (HM Treasury 2004)
- Parenting debates – the importance of parenting and support for those in difficulties and a significant focus on adoption and children looked after through the Quality Protects agenda (DoH, 1998).

These wider structural policies have been developed into operational policy in terms of social work practice in the *Every Child Matters* (DoH, 2003) agenda for change, reinforcing the concepts of universal services and early intervention and a more hands-on approach for those parents/children requiring a higher level of support via targeted intervention. These services are located and delivered within an ecological framework (Bronfenbrenner, 1979) and aimed at the five priority outcomes identified by children and young people:

- Being healthy
- Staying safe
- Enjoying and achieving
- Making a positive contribution
- Achieving economic well-being

The Children Act 2004, with its emphasis on preventative approaches and inter-professional working, provides the 'legislative spine' for the wider strategy of improving children's lives and the radical changes in the delivery and organisation of children's services (Blewett, Lewis and Tunstill, 2007; DfES, 2004).

Relationship-based versus bureau-professional social work practitioners

Another noticeable shift that has occurred over the past two decades and impacted on childcare social work has been the move away from traditional relationship-based social work to a more bureaucratised case management role. As a result of this shift a tension has developed for both the social work profession and individual practitioners about how core values can be operationalised.

Social workers tend to be defined by *who* – the organisation – they work for rather than *what* they do. Being a social worker tends to be synonymous with working for a local authority (Blewett *et al.*, 2007; Halmos, 1995) and the tensions of professional practice are probably greater in this area than in a voluntary organisation, due to the proliferation of organisational imperatives and policy guidelines. As a consequence, whilst practitioners may wish to be creative and innovative in their practice, the opportunity to exercise professional discretion and innovation are generally more restricted within the statutory sector. Blewett *et al.* (2007), however, offer a ray of hope, arguing that the proposed changes within the Every Child Matters agenda afford some opportunities to reduce these tensions and reclaim core values.

Tensions in contemporary childcare social work

Having outlined the broader socio-political context of current childcare social work characterised by a preoccupation with risk, the growth in significance of market forces and mixed economies of care and challenges to professional identity, it is possible to explore some of the tensions embedded in this context under four broad headings:

- Regulation and accountability
- Managerialism
- Explanation-orientated, evidence-informed practice
- Supervision, surveillance and innovation

Regulation and accountability

The process of regulation, closely connected to the notion of risk and interest in market forces, started in 1997 with the Government's Best Value initiative, which was introduced to ensure local authorities exercised their duties in an *effective, efficient and economic* way. A central component of these regulatory systems is the focus on quality in the provision of services and much attention has been focussed upon the construction of standards for practitioners to adhere to and tools that measure how well individual or organisations have performed. The National Occupational Standards (GSCC, 2002) and the PQ framework (GSCC, 2005) are just such benchmarks against which practice is measured. This preoccupation with regulation and quality assurance measures is clearly evident at an organisational level in the operational targets and performance indicators set for local authorities and the star ratings given for achieving them and at a practitioner level in the introduction of performance-related pay.

Such measurement devices could be argued as constituting an attack on professional accountability, in that rigorous standardisation can limit creativity and deny the anxieties and variability present within the practice environment. Conversely, Eby (2000) argues that such benchmarks are a necessary and effective measure of practice and that the emphasis should be on developing practitioners who can innovate within a regulatory system. What is abundantly clear is that conflict can and does

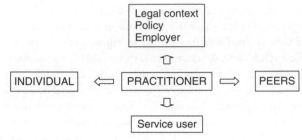

Figure 10.1   Stakeholder-related practice tensions

arise between different stakeholders and different benchmarks. Wonnacot (1993:??) describes these continually shifting tensions as 'the amoebic world of practice' where practitioners are continually pulled in different directions transforming the shape and the nature of their practice. These tensions can be seen in Figure 10.1 which demonstrates the need for the practitioner to balance the tensions of accountability between stakeholders.

One of the consequences of increased regulation is a concurrent growth in accountability and proceduralisation. Being regulated by implication means being accountable, which in turn requires procedures and systems – all part of the growth of managerialism in contemporary practice.

Managerialism

The increased influence of risk on welfare practices in recent years and the regulatory frameworks that it generates have been the main reasons for the emergence of practice that is dominated by bureaucratic, managerially defined responses and for childcare practice that is characterised less by the exercise of professional judgment than it is by the need to follow rules and procedures (Howe, 1992; Munro, 2004). According to Sheppard (1995) the balance between rules and procedures and professional judgement has fundamentally shifted and this in turn has brought into question the professional status of social work. The balance of power has shifted to managers, who are now the dominant voice of social work – both managers who control the nature of the professionals work and managers who hold the bureau-professional power.

As a direct result of this 'jurisdictional dispute' (Abbot, 1988) over the nature of social work, it is increasingly difficult for the more valued aspects of the task, such as direct work with service users or challenging aspects of social justice, to be recognised and prioritised. Evidence to support this argument can be found in statistics that illustrate the shift in professional activities amongst childcare social workers. In the early 1990s, it was estimated that a childcare social worker would spend approximately 15% of their time on bureaucratic tasks (Prince, 1993), thus spending 85% of their time face to face with service users. In 2006 Statham estimated that 25–33% of time was spent with service users. The Children in Need survey (DoH, 2000) was more generous, estimating about 66% of a practitioner's time was spent face-to-face with families, although this percentage included time spent writing assessment reports and evaluations. Over the past 15 years this would indicate there has been a significant reduction in time spent directly working with children and families of between 20 and 60% and that the increased proceduralisation of practice means that within these time allowances there is less opportunity for practitioners to exercise professional judgements.

A further consequence of the emergence of managerialism in practice is reflected in organisational expectations that understand practice-related issues as resolvable in a calculative logical manner (Parton, 1995). A corollary of this expectation is the devaluing of and restricted opportunities for creative judgements. Collings and Murray (1996) attribute this to be one cause of social work stress. Ongoing difficulties of retention in childcare practice could also be seen as a result of the difficulties in reaching workload targets coupled with expanding administration.

Managerial practices, accountability and proceduralism, however, should not be seen entirely negatively. On a positive note, procedures provide clear lines of accountability enabling practitioners to know what is expected of them, they allow for closer scrutiny of the social work task and may provide some consistency for the service user. They must, however, be handled with care to avoid the risks of managerialism identified by Lymbery and Butler (2004:61):

The relentlessness of practice and ethical conflicts within bureaucratised and insensitive organisations leave many social workers demoralised and propelled into defining themselves as victims – epitomised by defensiveness, routinised responses and reactive, rather than proactive, approaches to practice.

Evidence-informed or evidence-driven practice?

The emergence of evidence-based or informed practice as another, relatively new, characteristic of contemporary childcare social work can be seen to have developed, like regulatory frameworks and managerialism, in response to concerns about risk. The concept of evidence-informed practice is borrowed from medicine and involves the conscientious, explicit and judicious use of current evidence to inform decision-making both in terms of interventions and outcomes and wider social problems (Sheldon, 2001; 2005). The current drive for technical-rational approaches to decision-making (Schon, 1991), which is a central component of evidenced-based or informed practice within social work, can be understood as an attempt to eliminate risk and establish certainty in practice interventions and outcomes. Evidence-informed practice, however, is by no means a straightforward concept and in embracing it practitioners need to exert professional judgment and caution (Webb, 2001). Practitioners need to be aware that terms such as 'research mindedness' and 'research-based practice' operate along a continuum between the positivist stance associated with the ideas of Sheldon at one end and Webb's more qualitative position at the other end.

One important source of support that can contribute to practitioners developing a discerning stance towards evidence and which can play a key role in the creation of another equally significant source of practice knowledge – 'practice-informed evidence' – is supervision. Unfortunately the role and function of supervision, like the other aspects of professional practice discussed earlier, is similarly under threat from the excesses of managerialism see Chapter 3.

Surveillance, supervision and innovation

Supervision is probably the main tool for monitoring and measuring standards and developing creative and innovatory practice. It can be an effective mechanism for holding and mediating the tensions inherent in practice (Figure 10.2) and effective supervision should enable practitioners to reach a balance between case management and case development. There remains inherent conflict in the nature of supervision, however, as the agenda for each participant holds a different focus. For the supervisor it is about case management, standards and targets, for the supervisee the focus is on developing their practice. Both are tied by the constraints of the organisation (Eby, 2002). It is widely recognised that there has been a gradual but continuous shift away from the supportive and development aspects of the supervision process and task towards increasingly managerial, case management forms of supervision (Ruch, 2007a).

In essence, the fundamental tension in the supervisory relationship is between surveillance and organisational control and innovation and individual practitioner professional development.

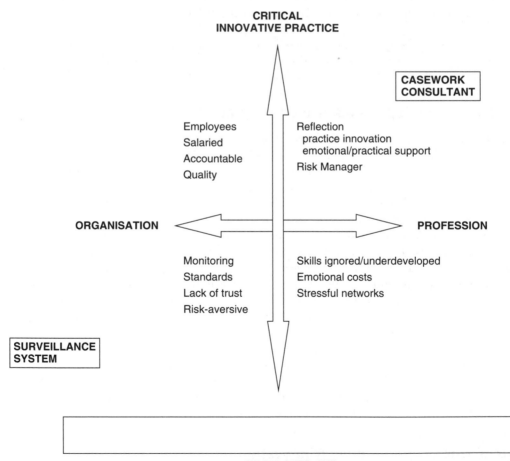

Figure 10.2   The optimum supervisory environment for innovative practice

The matrix in Figure represents these tensions. Practitioners for whom the content of supervision is characterised by the descriptors in the lower quadrant are likely to be practicing defensively and procedurally, whilst those whose supervision encompasses elements of the upper quadrant are likely to be more able to be innovative and creative within their practice. In an ideal practice context practitioners will find themselves located somewhere near the centre of the crossing axes. It is rare, however, for conventional individual supervisory structures to be able to meet all these demands. Effective learning organisations that value their employees recognise the diverse professionals needs of social work practitioners and the need to provide a range of support forums to meet them (Harrison and Ruch, 2007; Ruch, 2007b).

Learning points

- Practice within the children and families sector is inseparable from the political and regulatory forces that govern it. Over the past 20 years change has been ongoing and constant.
- Increased regulation has resulted in value tensions between individual practitioners, social work as a profession and the organisations in which they practice.
- The result of increased bureaucratisation means that the way in which practitioners relate to children and their families has changed and the time spent with them has decreased substantially.
- Supervision can offer the opportunity to effectively manage these tensions.

Reflective Activity

Think about what aspirations you had when becoming a social worker.

- Can you identify three changes in practice since you qualified that have created tensions for you as a practitioner?
- What has been the role of supervision in mediating those tensions?
- What other strategies have you used?

Holding on to innovation

Good practice requires innovation and creativity but such notions do not sit easily with the already identified phenomenon of risk regulation and managerialism and another associated concept – competence – which in recent years has come to dominate professional practice, at both qualifying and post-qualifying levels. Unsurprisingly, a competence framework fits well into the predominantly risk-averse, regulatory and managerialist culture with its ease of measurement and accountability. Not only does it provide some certainty in terms of the routines of practice and specified procedure, but it relies on the complexity of practice being reduced to procedures. This is in spite of the fact that such proceduralisation has not been shown to be any more successful at meeting service user needs and is less satisfying for the practitioner (Lymbery, 2003). A consequence of following procedures is the loss of innovation and awareness of social work as profession. The inclination to take refuge in procedures comes as a shock to many practitioners entering the profession but is experienced as a necessary stance, given the constraints of everyday practice:

> Many practitioners are shocked to find themselves in forms of practice dominated by – depending on the location – financial management, bureaucratization and proceduralisation.
>
> (Lymbery, 2003:104)

It has been argued that focusing purely on a competence framework oversimplifies the social work task (Clarke, 1995; Lymbery, 2003; Parton, 2006). Whilst at qualifying levels, a competence framework is probably sufficient, it is inadequate in more complex areas of practice or at post-qualifying levels of training. It is at this level and within assessment and evaluation that the potential for creativity is at its greatest. Sheppard (1995) divides the professional role into two:

- The technical rational aspects of the role (competence)
- Ability to use judgement (creativity)

The increased focus on competence has a number of dangers for both practice and social work as a profession as it risks:

- Creating a passive professional
- Encouraging defensive proceduralised practice
- Decreasing the sense of commitment and identity
- Limiting the ability to exercise professional judgement

Clarke (1998) argues that the problems faced by social workers in daily practice are *'sufficiently unfamiliar, complex and subtle to require the application of creativity and imagination to resolve them'*. Competence, therefore, is necessary but not sufficient for professional practice. Blewett *et al.* (2007) underline the difficulty of separating the concepts of role and task and the political context debates about improving practice. Creativity and innovation in practice is not just about new and exciting ideas for practice. It is about decisions and suggestions that occur in the complex and challenging realities of everyday practice, the ability to synthesise information from a unique situation into an empowering practice intervention and the capacity to think 'outside the book' (SUIG, 2006). Clarke (1998) views social work as a discipline rather than a profession combining the notions of competence and creativity to achieve best practice. Holding onto innovation has been a difficult task for many practitioners. Value conflict between the organizations they work in and their own practice values, limited resources, increasingly high workloads and increased bureaucracy has led practitioners to leave childcare social work or adjust their practice in a non-challenging and passive way. According to Charles (2004:181):

> the social worker is in the middle of a tug-of-war wrenched in one direction by professional knowledge, skills and values relating to the nurturing aspects of practice and hauled in the other by the economic, regulatory demands and bureaucratic controls of the organisations. Freedom of manoeuvre is limited by these managerialist forces…

Whilst the impact of organisational change and culture should not be underestimated there is scope for creativity and self-determination and developing ways of managing the tension between bureaucratic requirements and professional integrity (Parton, 1996). Hatton (2007) proposes a definition of creativity that incorporates the desire to improve practice and to create new forms of practice. He draws heavily on European influences of pedagogy to revisit relationship-based social work and describes creativity as having three central elements:

- To modify existing ways of doing things to make them more relevant to people providing and experiencing services
- To challenge current ways of doing things and in particular to expose the limitations of forms of practice which focus on outcomes and which neglect relationships as an integral part of practice
- To develop new ways of doing things which build on the best elements of current practice but which also draw on European traditions of pedagogy and social pedagogy

(Hatton, 2007:3)

How then can practitioners hold on to innovation and creativity in their practice?

Personal power

In spite of incessant organisational demands practitioners have retained considerable autonomy over their time and workload. Consequently, they can maintain and develop their personal power to identify and work with cases in their preferred style, thus benefiting the worker and service user and managing risk for the organization. Creativity and innovation are increased as the worker is using their preferred style and challenges to individual belief systems and organisational tensions are made after critical reflection of the circumstances and in the worker's timescales.

One example of a practitioner exerting personal–professional power was provided by a PQ candidate who talked about how she had revised the way she conducted core assessments in line with her experience of undertaking child observations. Instead of restricting her involvement with a family to question-and-answer interviews to gather the necessary information required by the Framework for Assessment she undertook two observational visits to the family which provided a wealth of data which helped her understand the concerns expressed about the family and informed her subsequent discussion with them. Whilst initially fearful of this approach being more time consuming this practitioner quickly realised she had gathered far more information than she would have in conventional interviews which would have taken as long or longer, and that having gathered this information she was able to be more focussed and efficient in the assessment interviews with the family.

Reflection

The central role of reflective practice for both effective practice and practitioner well-being has been discussed in Chapters 3 and 9. In the context of the constraints of regulation and risk-averse approaches to professional practice the importance of practitioners acquiring well-honed reflective capabilities is heightened. The ability to reflect is necessary for professional survival. Failure to reflect upon the impact and experience of practice leads to decreased efficiency, increased reliance on procedures and eventually stress, with its concomitant impact on staff well-being and retention.

Morrison (1996), drawing on the ideas of Summit (1983), applies the social work accommodation cycle to practitioners who become trapped in unsatisfactory practice environments. When faced with challenges to practice workers adopt one of two positions: either they reflect and take action or they enter a cycle of accommodation where they hide their true feelings or fail to recognise them. Morrison refers to the latter response as 'secrecy', a behaviour that leads to decreased emotional proximity. Workers operating under the conditions of 'secrecy' take frequent sick leave, deny or fail to recognise the extent of workplace and societal oppression or in the face of difficulties take a heroic position of trying harder. This is particularly true of females within organisations who work harder to gain approval and become resentful when efforts are not recognised. Once the accommodation cycle is entered reflective practice and supervision are put on hold to cope with yet another crisis and so begins a downward spiral of lost energy and defensive practice (Lymbery and Butler, 2004)

Perhaps the biggest challenge of practitioners lies in organisational resistance and obstacles to the development of reflective practitioners. On more than one occasion I have been told by PQ candidates, following their experience on the PQ programme of case discussion forums, of their attempts to introduce similar forums in their teams only to find their efforts undermined by team managers who fail to see their benefits and simply consider them an ineffective use of time and scarce resources. Encouraging frontline managers to recognise the value of reflective forums, such as those referred to in Chapter 3, and to facilitate their introduction, needs to be a priority of PQ Programme providers in conjunction with PQ candidates.

Supervision and professional development

Historically supervision has always been considered the primary forum for professional development (Kadushkin, 1976). As stated earlier the quality of supervision has a significant impact upon practice, with 'ideal supervision' operating within the middle and upper right quadrant of Figure 10.2. With the demise of the more holistic models of supervision that addressed the management, support and development of practice the role and purpose of supervision needs to be reconsidered. The dominance of case management agendas within supervision is well documented and a continued source of resentment for practitioners who simply do not expect to have the opportunity to discuss the emotional impact of their work, despite this being increasingly widely recognised (Ferguson, 2005; Ruch, 2007a; Smith, 2000 and 2005). In line with the previous discussion of forums facilitating reflective practice, practitioners can maintain innovation and creativity by taking control of the supervisory agenda and looking for their needs to be met from more than one source such as through consultation, peer support and mentorship.

Practice evaluation

Evaluation is linked to the development of reflection and knowledge and should focus upon the quality not the quantity of work undertaken. A balanced reflection of strengths and weaknesses increases the potential for creative responses and limits the extent to which practice is characterised by routinisation (Sheppard, 1995). This can aid the individual practitioner in gaining a broader view, especially if wider stakeholder perspectives are also taken into consideration. Increasingly the views of service users can be heard strongly and consistently giving the message that they appreciate helping relationships in general (Blewett *et al.*, 2007; Thoburn *et al.*, 1995) and more specifically direct working with children and families. Blewett *et al.* (2007) argue that childcare practitioners need to be able to undertake, not just commission services, and this is evidenced by numerous service user voices (Morgan, 2006; ATD 4th World, 2006). Service users also demonstrate insight into the tensions betweens role and tasks that the practitioner encounters:

Young people recognised that social workers are often working in difficult stations that limit what they can do... they are often given different rules to follow in different councils, or in the same council, so they are not able to make decisions... that they had a difficult job, in general were overworked, not paid very well ... that there were not enough of them and they all needed smaller caseloads.

(Morgan, 2006:11)

The participation of service users and carers is firmly on the practice agenda and now a key feature in the role of social care services and the training of its workforce, beginning with the 1990 National Health Service and Community Care Act, followed by government directives and further reinforced by New Labour's modernising agenda. Whilst achieving much in principle there is less clear evidence regarding what changes have resulted in practice from increased participation (Doel *et al.*, 2007). Howe (1991) identifies two broad benefits to partnership working – political and therapeutic. Wade (2006) feels concentration on the impact of participation of young people is focussed upon the question 'Has this young person been actively listened to?' with a lesser focus upon 'Is there any evidence of changes in practice as a result?'

Within social work training generally, and the new PQ system in particular, the arrangements for service user and carer involvement are required to be comprehensive and integral to the design, delivery and assessment of the programme (GSCC, 2006). The Service User Inclusion Group (SUIG) at the University of Portsmouth is a group of approximately 40 service users, carers and young people. Initially formed in 2001 the group has grown in strength and purpose. One area of work where the group has had both political as well as therapeutic benefits is in the area of creative means of engagement. The group's views regarding the effectiveness of innovative and creative ways of engaging in learning and teaching, such as art, drama and creative writing, led to the development of the 'Create' project and a fundamental review of the teaching strategies used within programmes, challenging educators to use more creative mediums within their teaching and raising questions as to whether these methods would then result in more creative practitioners. Drawing heavily on social pedagogic principles of 'the common third' by using specific tools or activities as a route to engagement and reinforcing previous service user research regarding the significance of relationship-based practice and skilled communication (Morgan, 2006; Blewett *et al.*, 2007) the group has influenced the design and delivery of the units and is actively involved in assessment artefacts within the programme.

Service user and carer inclusion is underpinned by the core social work values of participation and empowerment, although involvement appears to exist along a continuum from tokenistic to active citizenship. Carr (2004) identifies a number of factors, which can facilitate active participation of which there appear to be four main strands:

- Willingness within organisations to respond to the voice of participants
- Open-mindedness to different ways of working
- Awareness of the power dynamics operating both on an organisational and individual practitioner level
- Systems are created to evaluate not just the experience for the participant but also the impact in terms of change

Learning points

- Creativity and innovation are necessary facets of good practice.
- Practice requires both competence and the ability to exercise professional judgement.
- Holding onto innovation and creativity is a continuous challenge for practitioners.
- Practitioners need to be inclusive, reflexive and proactive to maintain innovation.
- Service users value practice that is individualised, innovative and creative.

Conclusion

This chapter has sought to stimulate discussion and thinking around the challenges and opportunities present in childcare practice on a political, organisational and individual level. Social work is constantly adapting to change and achieving a balance between socially liberal and socially authoritarian approaches. Whilst what social work has to offer has not changed the context in which it operates, it has seen practice shape and reshape itself in response to different political climates. The move to technocratic approaches, which appears impressive, has been to differing degrees bureaucratically oppressive. There is a growing recognition that more clearly measurable practice does not necessarily equate to better practice outcomes (Gupta and Blewett, 2007). Such approaches have increased the tensions between core professional values and the state. The inability to manage these tensions has resulted, first, in recruitment and retention difficulties within the profession and, secondly, in a heightened risk of practitioners being caught in a cycle of accommodating behaviour, which has the effect of limiting creativity in practice. Lymbery and Butler (2004) argue the secret to liberation from the technical bureaucratic straightjacket and into child-centred practice lies in relationship-building and effective communication. It is possible for practitioners to develop and maintain innovatory and creative practice, indeed returning to the quote at the beginning of the chapter, this is exactly what professional practice involves, and what this chapter has sought to promote.

Chapter summary

- Social work roles and tasks – increased regulation and technocratic approaches have threatened traditional relationship-based nature of social work. Social work has a crucial role to play in the delivery of services not just the commissioning of them. It is this first-hand experience and mode of delivery that makes social work unique and service users feel to be most beneficial.

- Reactive versus proactive practice – there are historical and ongoing tensions between supporting families and protecting children. Despite legislation and policy to the contrary, practice realities are that workers are often confronted with crises rather than opportunities to intervene earlier within the community.
- Individual and community advocacy – *two* facets traditional to the social work role, namely relationship-based work as discussed above and radical community roles, have been eroded and challenged by the increased regulation and proceduralisation of practice, resulting in value tensions between professionals and employers.
- Risk – risk has been a major focus of regulation and the search for certainty in an uncertain world, the consequence of which has been the recognition of a risk society and an increasingly risk-averse practice environment.
- Innovation and creativity – experience and complexity within the practice environment provide optimum opportunities for creativity within the frameworks by which practice is governed. Creativity can be cultivated within regulatory and bureaucratic contexts to modify, challenge and develop new ways of doing things.

Reflective questions

How do you as a practitioner manage the tensions between stakeholders, i.e. the expectations of the state, families, other professionals, your agency?

Of the obstacles to creative and innovative practice identified in the chapter which would you identify as the biggest one in your work context?

How do you protect the freedom for professional creativity? What strategies do you use and could you use?

Chapter 11

Collaborative practice and its complexity

Chris Warren-Adamson

Chapter learning aims

- To develop an understanding of inter-professional and inter-agency practice in relation to the work of your organisation
- To explore the development of professional negotiations and partnerships
- To develop an understanding of 'community' as a site of contemporary social work intervention with an emphasis on innovative forms of professional practice
- To be able to interpret and endorse developments in inter-professional and inter-agency practice

Introduction

This chapter introduces theoretical ideas for practice, which embrace networking, inter-professional practice, effective communication and mobilisation of the resources of agencies working in tandem. A central assumption of the discussion is that Every Child Matters (ECM) represents yet another attempt to create a safer community of care. It embraces the personal, the inter-personal and the contextual and the structural. It is self-evidently a domain of great complexity. For example, it not only tackles the complexity of inter-professional practice but also tackles diversity and links the formal and the informal. The challenge of this domain of study is to examine and rehearse some of the collaborative processes involved in practice which link the formal (education, welfare, health, police, etc.) and the emergent professional world of child care work – early education practice (nursery, crèche work, etc.), home visiting, parent and family groups, parent education, children and family centre practice, stranger and kinship carers, community and neighbourhood initiatives, family group conference and community forum practice, social and adult education, and so on. It requires a paradigm for enquiry and a practice framework.

In Chapter 5 which discussed the structural basis of inter-agency and inter-professional practices, I argued that insufficient acknowledgement has been paid to the complexity of change and human behavioural resistance to collaborative practice. I proposed a number of challenges as follows:

- Denial – don't think about it and it will disappear
- Avoidance – you know it is there but bypass it and or make excuses in order not to deal with it
- Projection – casting one's own feelings onto others
- Reaction formation – a response whereby an individual takes on the behaviours of the people with whom they are in conflict
- Counterphobia – denying anxiety by adopting an aggressive stance
- Displacement – rather than take it out on the person who is causing us grief, take it out on another
- Reflected blame – allied to the above, reflected blame places these feelings on another to avoid receiving it oneself
- Rationalising or intellectualising – taking the emotion out of the transaction and concentrate on the factual material, the detail
- Escalation – blowing something out of proportion

Much of this behaviour has its roots in insecure sites of practice. For example, as part of the enquiry into this domain, and prior to paradigm building, it is important to be aware of a growing debate in the literature about the makings of disproportionate anxiety for children and family practitioners (Menzies, 1970; Menzies-Lyth, 1989) associated with the impact of an unmanageable audit and blame culture, proceduralism, reductionism and professionals under pressure, all of which are well-documented characteristics of contemporary professional practice (Balloch *et al.*, 1988; Norris, 1990; Smith, 2000/2005; Warren-Adamson, 2005; Heap, 2005). Also, there is the burden of bureaucracy and the cry to return to values (Caulkin, 2006) and a growing articulation of the need to re-instate relationship into practice (Ruch, 2007; Ferguson, 2005). Menzies-Lyth's observations about nursing teams has a particular relevance for child and family practitioners who express the same anxiety spectrum – drowning or keeping it at bay, splitting, triangles, flight, displacement, control, denial (Taylor *et al.*, 2007). Haigh (1999) and Shuttleworth (1991) add richness to a debate which makes us question seriously whether practitioners are just as ill-contained as the parents with whom they work. Stability and a strong motivation to engage over time appear critical in Inter-professional Education/Inter-agency (IPE/IA) practice.

The theoretical framework informing this chapter draws on the work of Cooper, Braye and Geyer (2004) – complexity and inter-professional education – which implies a substantial degree of self-organisation in learning, and hence the collaborative enquiry model. What is proposed is learning based on a collaborative enquiry group, with an expectation that each candidate develops the confidence to set up and critically evaluate their own collaborative enquiry group, consisting of a suitable range of ECM practitioners in the candidate's patch. First, what is a collaborative enquiry group?

Setting up a collaborative enquiry group

Collaborative or co-operative enquiry has a growing band of adherents (Heron and Reason, 2001; Baldwin, 2001; Healy, 2001; Gardner, 2003; Murphy, 2004; Moffat *et al.*, 2005; Harm and Westhuizen, 2006; Warren-Adamson, 2007). Commonly based on a group of around 6–8 people, it:

- Is participative and egalitarian in principle
- Acknowledges and tries to deal with subjectivity
- Occupies an epistemological stance between social realism and social constructionism
- Tends towards qualitative data and thick description

Groups develop through recognisable stages, and high levels of trust and self-organisation are likely to realise the strongest data. Hence, groups need to last beyond six months to gather momentum and are equally likely to lose momentum after, say, 18 months. It does depend on the quality of the group process. Groups also vary in their style and level of organisation. Thus far is the exciting bit. The trouble is, getting together as a grass-roots group with a will to explore knowledge that together may take you everywhere or nowhere. You will need permission. You will need a structure, an agenda, partly imposed by the programme you are involved in, and partly determined by the group. You will need leadership, often determined initially by rotation, meeting by meeting. Later, one or two of you will emerge with a leadership style that the group accepts. Then, how do you make sense of the findings or outcomes? There are the more straightforward process outcomes – friendship and new social relationships, trust, enjoyment, wanting to collaborate, the stimulation of new knowledge about each other's world. There are distal outcomes – what the outside world, the programme wants you to know and experience, usually written down. Then there are the synergistic outcomes, the generation of which involve the need to understand interdependencies, be sensitive to dimensions of relationships, focus on non-linearities, look for the unexpected, focus on processes, recognise dynamics, describe patterns as well as events, and so on (Anderson *et al.*, 2005). The chances are that, for example, bringing together a health visitor, a social worker, a sure start worker, a carer and teachers may generate perspectives that are new and surprising. Recording is the key. Minimally, a round-robin system of taking brief notes and a handful of proposals about what went on, which you can debate. Ideally, audio-recording and taking it in turns to do a full transcript which can be collectively analysed and debated. Of course, all the usual group rules apply but note that insecurity and 'paranoia' may be amplified in the IA/IP context and exchanging transcripts needs strict protocols and very careful attention.

Reflective Activity

BegintothinkabouthowyoucouldsetupacollaborativeenquirygroupasabaseforIA/IPlearning:

- As a course-based action learning set

or

- In your practice constituency with a course tutor as consultant

---

Complexity theory: a theoretical framework for inter-professional and network building practice

Cooper, Braye and Geyer (2004) claim that a difficult starting point in the study of inter-professional and network building practice is that (a) its advocates largely base their argument on a spurious 'common sense' argument and (b) the argument is linear, an approach which, despite an alternative paradigm having been recognised in the natural sciences for a considerable period of time, dominates social policy and social science thinking. Cooper *et al.* observe that improved communication between professionals and the organisations in which they are employed have long been argued as one of the key factors in the improvement of services. It underpinned Seebohm and finds a new expression in Every Child Matters and demands for IPE. It was also implicit in the Curtis Report (HMSO, 1946) which propelled the setting up of the post-war children departments and made sure that the newly appointed children's officers had a grass-roots knowledge of their charges and were also of equal status to the then local authority chief officers. Yet, such restructuring is highly contested, not least in social policy (for example, Kirkpatrick, 1999; Williams, 2004). Instead, Cooper *et al.* propose that complexity theory provides a more analytic framework to consider IPE/IA.

Complexity theory, a contemporary evolution from chaos theory, is the study of complex systems and is concerned with transformations – negative and positive – which arise from the fusion of biological activity. Complexity theory engages the tantalising idea that understanding the link between a transformed 'whole' and its original constituent parts is not easily made. *Complex systems* – weather, the Middle East, the brain, for example – to keep it on planet earth – are irreducible or at least difficult to dis-aggregate, and can be distinguished from *complicated systems* – for example the motor car, laptop, hair dryer, electric toothbrush – which can – by and large – be reduced from their recognisable states (motor car) and then be reassembled to that same state (motor car). In this domain, therefore, complex is different from complicated.

Systems and emergence

Complexity theorists talk of emergence, generally the appearance of higher-level features of a system, where, for example, a children's centre is an emergent feature of its component parts.

Apparently simple parts can lead to emergent complexity – e.g. from atoms to water. Apparently complex parts can lead to emergent simplicity – e.g. the orbiting moon. Complexity is about the way the world works: it is about relationships. Synergy is the next step – it concerns co-operative behaviour resulting in transformation.

Synergy

Synergy derives from the Greek 'sunergos' 'The whole is greater than the parts', the whole is **different** than the parts and the whole can do things that the parts cannot. The parts may be unaware or only partly aware of their contribution to the whole. Synergy involves transformation, and synergy is everywhere (Corning, 1996), from the aggregation of sub-atomic particles to the collective endeavours of women and men. A collaborative ECM group will seek to develop synergy, something more than its membership. With synergy, there is a flowering of interest in symbiosis, defined as a beneficial close association between two or more organisms.

Complexity and self-organisation

Complex systems are said to have a self-organising capability (autopoiesis) and can change spontaneously according to or despite the intentions of the agents within the system. It means unpredictability and small changes can have big impacts. Moreover, it means that such systems may be too complex for agents to control or indeed understand.

Starlings

Complexity theorists offer vivid illumination in metaphor. David Whyte, poet and consultant to corporate America, presses us to consider the starling!

> *The starlings drove along like smoke...misty...without volition – now a circular area inclined in an arc...now a globe, now...a complete orb into an ellipse...and still it expands and condenses, some moments glimmering and shimmering, dim and shadowy, now thickening, deepening, blackening!*
>
> Coleridge 1779 (Cited in Whyte 2002:215–216)

This ordinary bird – *sturnus vulgaris* – in a flock has proximal instincts, to keep up, to keep distance, to strive towards the middle and so on. The long-term outcome – despite the oblivious starling – is a glorious, glorious flocking. Whyte's strong advice is that efforts should not be made to control the flock but rather to understand, trust and encourage the constituent qualities of the birds in the flock, which is constantly transformative and unique.

The implication of this is that inter-professional, inter-agency, collaborative arrangements imply potentially complex systems, emerging into new synergies, and presenting yet another challenge for conventional management. The implication for learning is embraced in Toseys's work (2002). Drawing on Tosey, Cooper *et al.* construct a four-dimensional framework:

• Self-organisation – like the starlings, rather than control learning, facilitators are encouraged to create the conditions for learning rather than to direct and seek to control outcomes. Beautiful outcomes are negotiated and socially constructed.

- Paradox – examines the power between educator and students and emphasises its messiness, diversity of learning mode and outcomes. At the same time, it recognises that 'every educational act is also an act of governance' – programmes have intention, expectation of new knowledge and new levels of performance.
- Emergence – accounts for the manner in which a system behaves and develops its own qualities as emerging from local and apparently ill-co-ordinated activities. It implies that the heterogeneity in students' levels of learning should be recognised and nurtured, as small interventions can result in big changes, and vice versa.
- Operating at the edge of chaos – this implies that systems are at their most creative at the edge of chaos. Tosey says:

It is like a good party; lively, lots of flowing conversations, and fun. A party in stasis would be safe, but probably boring and stilted; one in chaos might be thrillingly anarchic, or perhaps offensive and dangerous. In chaos, a system could self-organise into a higher level of complexity ... or it could disintegrate.

The implications are that interventions together are unpredictable and surprising, but can be satisfactorily managed by strongly shared values.

Reflective Activity

Complexity theory provides a serious challenge to professional and quasi-professional life:

- Howmightemerginggroupsynergyanddifferencesinunderstandingaboutoutcomesconstitute a challenge to collaborative practice?

Learning points

- Anxiety and defensive professional reactions can result in simplistic responses to the complexities of inter-professional practice.
- To fully engage with inter-professional practice requires engaging with collaborative approaches and complexity.
- Collaborative enquiry groups offer a means of exploring, promoting and facilitating collaborative professional practice.
- Complexity theory offers a helpful, but challenging, theoretical and conceptual framework for responding to the demands of inter-professional practice.

The eco-systemic perspective: a framework for theorising human behaviour across systems

A big paradigm shift in understanding has been represented in Bronfenbrenner's ecological perspective where human behaviour is explained in terms of a set of ever widening, nested systems,

(Bronfenbrenner, 1979). In the US it shaped theorising about practice (perhaps less so practice itself) but took its time in the UK until getting formal recognition in the Government's Framework for the Assessment of Children in Need (HMSO, 2000).

Bronfenbrenner (1979) was not the first to develop a dynamic systemic perspective of child development (Sugarman, 1986) but his nested systems saw a resurgence and quick acceptance. The original framework saw the child's immediate system as a micro system, embedded within an exo-system wherein Bronfenbrenner located school, work and all that touches upon the child and her family in the day to day. All of that is located within a macro system, the broad, global, meta-cultural system. And all are inextricably linked. Such linkages are termed a 'meso system', for example, Bronfenbrenner's enduring example is the family and school. Nothing stands still, however, and Figure 11.1 is an elaboration of Bronfenbrenner's nested systems.

Moreover, ground-breaking research in genetics, neurology and the brain is encouraging us to integrate further and to talk of a seamless bio-psycho-social perspective. Nowhere is that more

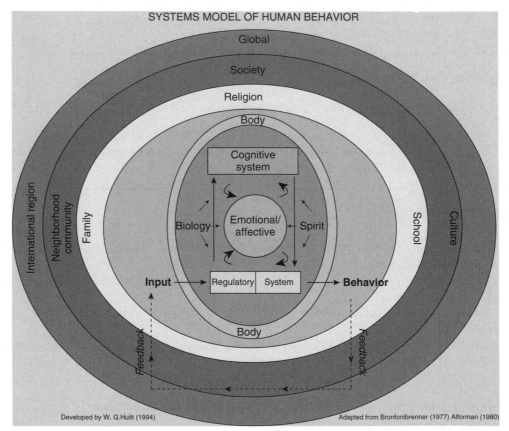

Figure 11.1 An adaptation of Bronfenbrenner's Ecological Systems

demonstrated than in current practice in mental health services (Shore, 2001; Gerhardt, 2004). Some of the implications of this framework for IPE/IA thinking are as follows:

Context   To describe the child's developmental trajectory in these terms is to embrace context, including exclusion and impoverishment, as well as biology and psyche. However, embracing context is not without its challenges – for example, the Framework for Assessment has its critics (Calder, 2003). Not least, office- or bureau-based sites for practice make assessment particularly difficult when it comes to evaluating informal, hidden and intricate social support systems.

Linkage   It is the meso-systemic thinking which is critical in this framework and necessary for creating the satisfactory links for example, between parent and child individuation, family and school, close and wider attachments.

Social support   Research and theorisation which gives encouragement to the idea of social support intervention is long established. For example, Whittaker, Schinke and Gilchrist (1986) write about *practice* and the idea of social networks as '*personal communities*' which reflect (a) involvement in the major spheres of life, (b) the degree and manner in which these spheres are integrated or segregated and, (c) the values and choices by which human beings seek to achieve meaningful participation in their culture, society, and community (Hirsch, 1981).

Formality and informality   Concepts of life-span theory assume that the family is not a closed unit but, over the course of the life cycle, it is enhanced by, is interdependent with, and is part of the wider community as a social support network. Such a social support network is constructed through participation in organisations of varying degrees of formality and informality (Whittaker, 1986)
    Formality is defined as follows: (a) hierarchical levels of authority that govern decision-making and communication, (b) specialisation of functions as reflected in job titles, (c) organisational roles in which occupants are replaceable, (d) role relations based on what people do and (e) rules, policies and procedures that cover the operations of the organisation and the work behaviour of its personnel.
    In contrast, informal systems develop spontaneously – networks of face-to-face relationships, personal and collective satisfactions. Social support, whether formal or informal, is transactional, mediated by what the person does and how receptive she/he is to the efforts of others, and the environmental context (Coyne and Holroyd, 1982) and, of course, social support systems are not *necessarily* supportive.
    Formal and informal structures (Germain, 1991) can be elaborated as follows:

- Formal, complex bureaucratic organisations
- Informal systems in formal organisations – subsystems of formal organisations have certain properties parallel to those of the formal system
- Community organisation relations – formal organisations need community information and should be shaped to meet community needs
- Formed group – still have rules and structure, a measure of formality – but they are not as formalised as bureaucratic organisations
- Self-help groups – can be expressive (that is primarily concerned with members support) or instrumental (that is concerned with external goals)

natural helping	mutual aid	self-help groups	assigned peer helpers	assigned non-peer helpers	professionals

More	Training increasing	Social More	distance formality more	and structure formal *Status less hands on Home life more*	Matching *seeking diagnostic boundaried*

Figure 11.2　Formal and informal patterns of intervention

- Social networks – relatives/kin, neighbours and friends – each serve different functions, as follows: neighbours (short-term emergency), kin (long-term commitment), friends (guidance, affirmation, emotional support).

Within this continuum, intervention also reflects degrees of formality. Practitioners and helpers are characterised on the one hand by training and distance and on the other by no training and close engagement, all occupying the same terrain. Figure 11.2 elaborates on these different types of intervention.

Complexity, linkages between people and systems, formality and informality, are arguably critical ideas that are now carried into a discussion about how best to develop systems of care.

Reflective Activity

Eco-systemic theory and its implication for linkages:

- How does the idea of spectrum of formal and informal activity challenge collaborative practice?

Towards a community or culture of care

The idea of the development of an integrated system of care based on a geographic location (Stroul, 1996), along with a parallel concept of wraparound care (Van Den Burgh and Grealish, 1986) are contemporary imports from the US. Strength-based, individualised planning, within the context of the above, has become broadly adopted in US initiatives of multi-agency care. That experience and those principles are worth exploring as the pressure on inter-professional and multi-agency practices grows with UK restructuring of children's services (Stevenson, 2005).

Klaehn and Martner (2003), in developing a conceptual framework for an early childhood system of care, have themselves adapted a framework which can be conceptualised as a child and young person's system of care. It provides us with a helpful start. In summary, they propose that such a model should:

Support the biological, psychological, and social development of children and families (author's adaptation)

Klaehn and Martner emphasise Winnicott's idea of the 'holding environment' (1965). The child is 'held' by her mother/caretaker in such a way that her early fragmented 'good and bad' behaviour is managed and over time reconciled by the emerging individual. Shuttleworth's (1991) account of 'containment' gives a more contemporary view. Originally focused on the parent-child dyad, it is argued that this idea can be widened to the system of care. The implication is profound for practitioners. Expectations of the containing practitioner/parent include long-term commitment, an instinctive wisdom, growing experience, having a containing world of their own, and managing the child's dependence, inter-dependence and independence according to the variabilities of need, and long into adulthood. These are serious challenges for an inter-professional and inter-agency system.

Make families full partners at every level

This applies to all levels, from case to social policy development. For example, it presses us to develop an easy and practiced familiarity with family group conferencing (Connelly, 1994; Nixon, 2001), but it does not have to stop there. Some FGC initiatives have built on the confidence gained by family members in FGC work to encourage children's and family forums, where the focus is upon, for example, collective problem-solving in neighbourhoods.

Provide support for the stability of children's families – biological, friends, adoptive, foster

Klaehn and Martner cite the pleasing title from the text *From Neurons to Neighbourhood* (2000) in its evidential support for supportive environments. The next step, however, is to examine the nature of stability, which is a challenge for professionals, semi-professionals and non-professionals who contribute to child care systems. Here too the emphasis is upon developing attachments and attachment opportunities for children. However, an increasingly mobile workforce is prone to leave attachment making to the least mobile and those with least capacity. Non-stability in the system is one of the greatest challenges and the debate will need to go beyond selective targeting of specific reforms – training, pay and status – to complex societal changes (see Novotny, 2005). Employers' attempts to lasso, constrain and regulate practice appears likely to aggravate the tendency to proceduralism, or flight, and therefore instability.

Formulate individualised and integrated multi-agency service plans with the full participation of the child's family

Much of the above implies the integration of, not least, the domestic economy, adult and child mental health needs, effective participation in and sometime overcoming neighbourhood and community constraints, safeguarding processes, and education. This is a rich configuration that requires practitioners to revisit their skills in case management where inexperience and instability dominate. It links with the formal/informal spectrum above.

Value and respect the family's unique social and cultural beliefs and interests in order to provide culturally competent and clinically appropriate services

A generation of commentary on inclusive practice and children with disabilities, cross-cultural and anti-racist practice, which have evolved in our appreciation of complexity, has probably not made practice any more confident in this domain. Collective negotiation within teams around dilemmas of disability, race and ethnicity, and containing rather than functional supervision, need to be combined with stability, experience and memory. The response of minority groups managing an unstable, memory-less, indigenous professional culture may have lessons for us.

Intervene without delay to meet the developmental needs of children

Better technologies and common assessment frameworks may contribute to efficient services but delay may also be caused by (a) anxiety and therefore lead to procrastination, (b) a culture which doubts the effectiveness of certain kinds of intervention (for example, the looked after system), (c) a lack of confidence, memory and experience of confident intervention amongst practitioners.

Ensure smooth transitions between service system elements as the child's developmental needs change

Critics talk of barriers to a seamless service and the need for a principle of 'wraparound' care. Practitioners will need to debate how their community of care can develop over time a culture of common ownership. Within such a culture, at case level, individual practitioners will need the confidence and support to bang on other doors, and someone of high rank will need to dedicate their time to advocate 'wraparound' when things break down.

Encourage professionals within the system of care to make advocating for the child and family their highest priority and strive for an ethical balance between protecting the rights of children and supporting the rights of parents.

I shall take these together since they are about advocacy and balancing child and parent. A wise paper from Jordan (1987) identified social worker practitioners claiming to be either therapists or advocates. Jordan observed, however, that the majority occupy a complex middle ground of negotiation and balancing interest. For most practitioners advocacy threatens long-term practitioner survival and therapeutic opportunities are scarce. In response to these tensions, Wolfensberger (1986) famously argued for citizen advocates who combined long-term relation building and speaking out and for clients. As a scheme it enjoyed some success in adult mental health. An examination of the life of citizen advocacy may have lessons for the formal/informal interface, the endurance of formal systems and the frailty of informal systems.

Reflective Activity

Developing a system of care and wraparound practice:

- Howcanyoupromotecollaborativepracticethatovercomesill-containingenvironments,over-reliance on technology, instability, inexperience and short memory?

Another challenge to collaborative practice is the way in which interventions are shaped and change is facilitated.

Exchanging ideas on the construction of a theory of change and preferred models of intervention

A growing requirement from funders of social interventions is a statement about a theory of change, or put more simply, what are your interventions, what are your proposed outcomes and how do they connect? Evidently, professionals and emerging professionals have favoured interventions, explicitly and implicitly stated. A collaborative group would be advised to share knowledge and assumptions about change and interventions and the foregoing material should provide ideas and a structure.

In order to examine ideas about interventions, elsewhere (Lightburn and Warren-Adamson, 2006) a colleague and I have adapted an epistemological grid (Figure 11.3) borrowed from Howe (1987), in order to account for the varied helping relationships in children's and family centres, and framed these ideas as a set of negotiated agendas. Here, it is adapted again to examine the IPE/IA system of care. The grid is based on two continua, first between subjective knowledge and objective knowledge, and secondly ideas of society and change, based on consensus and conflict perspectives.

Such a perspective enabled Howe (1987) to propose four domains of intervention, which we have renamed:

- Regulatory, protective activity
- Personal development
- A collective world of learning, support and change
- Social change activities

In Figure 11.4, a grid to describe the parent and professional agendas in centres has been developed. The grid organises ideas about parent and professional agendas in four clusters. In each domain, services provided by the centre can be described in familiar ways. For example, in the *regulatory, protective activities* parents bring complex and hard-to-solve issues that are often tied to the

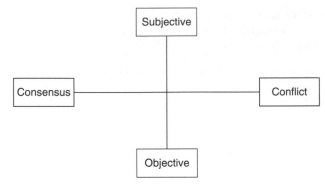

Figure 11.3 Four epistemological perspectives on the social work role

professional's duty to influence positive parenting and protect children. Conventional interventions include crisis intervention and parenting programmes. The domain of *personal development* would include therapeutic activities; for example, parents aspire to change – from the elimination of destructive, sometimes dangerous behaviours to all manner of self-development. Conventional interventions include counselling, psychotherapy, and so on. The domain of the *collective world of support and learning* occupies a spectrum of activities from adult education to group support and care. The fourth domain reflects parents' growth and engagement in social and community action.

This grid is useful starting point for professionals to examine their location, practice ideology and preferred intervention, although integration of practices and cross-overs and adaptation make it a contentious exercise. Moreover, whilst there is greater integration of theories of intervention, behaviour and child development, practitioners of particular disciplines nonetheless tend towards favoured theoretical perspectives, which may not only fit purpose and assumptions about change, but also concern professional niche, status, managing, self-protection. Inviting practitioners to sculpt their position in such a grid starkly lays bare these issues. Two problematic factors are singled out for special attention.

First, the study of centres, in particular, added further complication since it became clear that the grid by no means accounted for the change process. Synergy, the 'more than the sum of its parts' phenomenon, also contributes in a poorly understood way to the change process. Second, a further

Personal development Counselling, psychotherapy, progressive education	*Collective world of support and learning* Informal and adult education, empowerment and Freirian practice, community education and feminist practice, settlement activity
Regulatory, protective activity CBT, assessment, regulatory action, parent groups and education, diagnostic practices	*Social change* Social action and community work, lobby and TU activity, social entrepreneurship

Figure 11.4 Diverse modes of social work intervention

complication is associated with outcomes and timescales for their achievement. In a study of community-based practices, Warren-Adamson and Lightburn (2006) determined three kinds of outcome:

- The distal or long-term outcome – as in the government's five outcomes underpinning the Every Child Matters agenda
- The proximal or step on the way to change
- The mediatory outcome.

Thus, a distal outcome might be being healthy (enjoying good physical and mental health and living a healthy lifestyle); a proximal outcome might be learning to manage (managing a child's challenging behaviour); a mediatory outcome might be a confident staff group (offering containment). Negotiating and agreeing proximal and mediatory outcomes and establishing causal links between them, is a problematic activity, which may most productively be undertaken by the partnership of stakeholders engaged in an intervention together.

Reflective Activity

The idea of a theory of change and the part played by practitioners' favoured interventions:

- How do you overcome differences in interventions in developing collaborative practice?

Sites and homes for professional practice

The significance of practice site or professional home in inter-professional work contexts should not be underestimated. In an inter-agency, inter-professional world practitioners move out from their professional base and together occupy a corner of the families' *social* world whilst carrying with us the attachment to, label and connotations of the professional base, along with the offer of potential services. There are a number of challenges. For some, their domain is closely tied to the families' social world. For others, first and foremost they draw an identity from strong institutional links – education, health, police, law. Inter-professional/inter-agency groupings could be said to occupy a joining spectrum from representative (emerging only partially from their home institution) to synergy, where commitment to the new group is high, and new behaviours are greater than the sum of the parts.

Case conferences may be said to occupy the R end of the spectrum, youth offending teams (depending on leadership and other chemistries) towards the middle. In recent years, some family

Representative-----------1----------------------2---------------------3---------------Synergy

Figure 11.5 A continuum of sites of social work practice

centres and some children centres have shown the capacity to occupy the S end of the spectrum. An example is Hess, McGowan and Botsko's (2003) account of the Center for Family Life in Brooklyn, New York, which 'combines community rootedness with a clinical sophistication' in promoting support, recreational challenge and family, including kinship, placement in a big New York neighbourhood. Here a life-long centre nurtures itself to nurture others, without forsaking a very high professional expectation. Sites for practice, and their encouragement of practitioner capacity, appear to be critical variables in enquiries into extending opportunities for children.

Reflective Activity

Sites for practice include bureau, day centre, residential centre, clinic, resource centre:

- How do practice sites determine collaborative practice?

Learning points

- Ecological perspectives on family and professional systems encourage the integration of the newly emergent formal and informal childcare networks.
- Communities and cultures of care in inter-professional practice need to embrace the dynamic and subtle needs of children and their families.
- Theories of change need to recognise the differing 'drivers' that influence professional practice.
- Inter-professional working has the potential to develop creative sites of practice and strategies for delivering services.

Conclusion

In summary, New Labour has continued governments' preoccupation with developing linkages between practitioners and their institutions. As Cooper *et al.* (2004) remind us, despite a century of thinking about complexity in the natural sciences, the approach to this domain has been mainly linear. This chapter has attempted to rise to this challenge and has outlined a theoretical agenda for collaborative enquiry amongst ECM practitioners, which involves a set of ideas about collaboration, complexity, systems and formality and informality, a culture of care, intervention and theories of change, sites for practice, group process and mindset. The following is a quote from a collaborative enquiry group comprised of eight practitioners engaged in kinship or family and friends care. It seems to sum up the serious challenge and complexity faced in seeking to cross boundaries but the enormous potential for creative and effective practice such opportunities offer:

Lastly, there is the Looked After System itself, not one system but a complex set of sub-systems each with its own gravitational pull like planets in a solar system. This has been one of the unexpected and striking lessons of this study, prompted by group-members use of the word 'mindset'. By definition mindset involves knowing and committing yourself to a practice direction. Knowledge and commitment drives it. Mindset makes things work. It is hard to break out of, and sometimes appears as a juggernaut with poor brakes and poor turning circle. Mindset contributes an explanation to a number of recognisable practice tensions – prevention/protection, parent/child, concurrency. What I began to observe was the way each subsystem (as I perceive them) involve, inter alia, a legal knowledge, a cultural pattern and power, a status, a belonging, a loyalty, and of course a commitment, all of which exercise a powerful gravitational pull, an anchor. It constrains what is also required of practitioners, which is a fluid movement between systems and deft application of opportunity for clients' fast changing needs.

(Warren-Adamson 2007)

Chapter summary

- Effective IP working requires skills and understanding that reaches far beyond familiarity with government policies and procedures.
- Practitioners need to be able to embrace complexity and the challenges of working with difference and diversity within the professional network.
- Inter-professional working needs to recognise the varied sites of practice and multi-faceted motivations for change and intervention associated with individual service users and the diverse professional groups.
- Collaborative enquiry groups have the potential to facilitate effective IP working practices.

Reflective questions

To what extent would you identify yourself as a collaborative professional? What is your evidence for your answer?

On a personal/professional level, what are the biggest obstacles you can identify for you as an individual to engaging in collaborative IP working?

Within your professional context which of the theoretical frameworks introduced in this chapter would most help you in developing a more collaborative working practices?

Part Three

Continuing professional
development and future directions

Chapter 12

The way ahead: reflective practice and relationships

Gillian Ruch

There is always a danger when concluding a piece of writing to try to neatly 'wrap up' and 'sign off' all that has gone before. Hence I have avoided using the word 'conclusion' in the title of the chapter, preferring to suggest that this book makes a partial contribution to the much bigger, ongoing process of professional development. Such 'dangers' are not confined to the academic/publishing world. As any childcare social worker knows, all too well, the completion of common assessment documentation, a court report or a foster carer assessment, for example, leaves a feeling that there is as much unwritten as written. People and human relationships defy being neatly packaged or pigeonholed. It is this complexity of human behaviour that makes social work the challenging profession that it is. The situation is further complicated, however, by the over-riding political and societal push to 'dumb down' human behaviour. As Chapter 10 illustrated, the marketisation of welfare and the proliferation of bureaucracy is driving practitioners to respond to service users as rational individuals whose difficulties will disappear with the provision of a 'care package'. Yet, Chapters 3, 7 and 11 all recognise that it is precisely because people are complex beings with emotional and personal histories that such interventions on their own are ineffective.

One of the key components of continuing professional development, that was introduced in Chapters 3 and 11 particularly, is learning to live with complexity, multiple perspectives and truths. It is not an easy professional skill to acquire, as the discussion in Chapter 3 on the emotional demands of practice and the different practice approaches and skills introduced in Chapter 9 illustrate, as certainty and absolutes often feel more comfortable and allow us to 'be in control'. Learning to live with uncertainty and risk, as Gully highlighted in Chapter 7, is a necessary part of child development and I would suggest it is a pivotal feature of continuing professional development too.

How then can I draw this book to a close without resorting to unrealistic and simplistic conclusions about future practice? One way is to identify the different relationships that practitioners need to develop, maintain and nurture for effective, reflective practice and to recognise them as alive and dynamic:

- *The social work professional identity and the self* – the personal and professional tension that needs to be kept alive with both aspects of the person being fully acknowledged. Sustaining and nourishing personal and professional awareness requires the sort of reflective forums identified in Chapter 3, forums which focus on surface and depth issues, the conscious and unconscious dynamics in professional relationships and which embrace the complexity that these relationships generate.
- *Social worker and service user* – perhaps one of the most helpful ways of ensuring this relationship remains just and empowering is by always recalling how fine a line it is between being a professional and being a service user. At the same time there needs to be an honest acknowledgement of professional expertise and power to ensure service user perspectives and participation does not become a hollow exercise. Qualified practitioners do have expertise that is different to the service users' 'expertise on their own lives'. Practitioners must exercise their expertise responsibly and not undervalue it or allow it to be undermined.
- *Social worker and the socio-political context* – as Chapters 10 and 11 highlight, the ecological model and its influence on government policies and procedures has had important repercussions for the conduct of child care social work practice, with practitioners having a heightened awareness of the importance of context for children and families. It is equally important for practitioners to recognise their own professional socio-political context and the constraints they experience on their professional practice and freedom. Practitioners need to voice their concerns when policies contradict professional principles and through developing the skills required to 'enable others' (see Chapter 6) empower colleagues to express their opinions too. Cree's (2007) recent book *Social Work: Voices from the Inside* has collated experiences of practitioners and service users and makes a similar point:

> Social workers need to stand up and be counted; we need to be clearer about what social work can, and cannot offer; we need to be willing to contribute to public debates about issues as diverse as offending and the impact of poverty on the lives of those who use social work services.
>
> (Cree and Davies, 2007:159)

In order for practitioners to continue to develop professionally, all of these inter- and intra-personal experiences need attending to. There are no easy or quick solutions to the tensions and challenges they face – what matters is to keep the dialogue alive. In Chapter 7, Gully refers to the cynicism and world-weariness with which practitioners frequently commence PQ programmes. I too experienced this cynicism from a candidate who contributed to the evaluation comments for the Unit I taught by stating 'I really enjoyed what you covered in the unit but none of it was relevant.' Initially, and unsurprisingly, on hearing the comments of the candidate on the usefulness of the unit I was deflated. It was only on reading the unit assignments that I was able to put this statement in perspective. In several of these assignments practitioners commented on how, in light of their learning from the unit, they felt both more empowered to get the support they needed for their practice and to explore feelings of failure, fear and frustration. This discovery confirmed that the acknowledgment of feelings in practice encourages the creation of 'different' relationships. The systemic approaches, explored in Chapter 9, endeavour to facilitate change by inviting service users to try to do something 'differently', with a clear emphasis on the difference only needing to be small. A practitioner working systemically with a family, for example, might invite a parent to try relating to a child 'slightly differently'. To suggest too big a change might be asking the family to take too big a risk. The change need only be small. In terms of my teaching I too needed to heed this systemic principle and to adjust my expectations of what I could realistically expect practitioners to take on board and 'do differently'. This realisation led me to the fourth and final relationship that is crucial for effective and reflective practice:

- *Social workers and managers* – practitioners need to ensure that managers provide the appropriate support for their professional development. Supervision needs to endorse and support the centrality of relationships in the regulated, managerial contexts of practice. Practitioners need to have the confidence to ask managers to 'do it differently' with them – to offer more relational supervision. A sound psychodynamic principle is that we can only establish meaningful relationships with services to the extent that we experience meaningful relationships with those in authority over us. In order to professionally care for service users we, as professionals, need to feel cared about (Ferguson, 2005).

Finally experience of qualifying and post-qualifying learning tells us that topic-based learning (knowledge acquisition) and conceptual frameworks (theorising practice) need to go hand-in-hand. Whilst practitioners tend to prefer developing their specialist knowledge, social work educators emphasise the importance of practitioners developing theoretical understanding. In writing this book we concluded that focussing on conceptual frameworks – reflective, observation-based and collaborative practice – would enable practitioners to develop skills in advanced criticality for practice. We believe that practitioners who are equipped with these skills can apply them to their diverse but specific areas of expertise – working with safeguarded children and children who are looked after, domestic violence, asylum seekers, care leavers, youth offenders and children with multiple and complex needs. It is our hope that, in the course of their professional development, practitioners will continue to deepen and broaden their conceptual understanding in the context of the complex web of relationships that characterises contemporary childcare social work practice.

Bibliography

Abbot, A. (1988) The *System of Professions*. Chicago: University of Chicago Press.

Adams, R. (2002) Social work processes. In Adams, R., Dominelli, L. and Payne, M. (eds), *Social Work, Themes, Issues and Critical Debates*. Basingstoke: Palgrave Macmillan, 249–266.

Alaszweski, A. and Manthorpe, J. (1998) Welfare agencies and risk: The missing link, *Health and Social Care in the Community*, 6:4–15.

Aldgate, J., Jones, D., Rose, W. and Jeffery, C. (eds) (2006) *The Developing World of the Child*. London: Jessica Kingsley.

Anderson, S. (2005) Interagency information sharing in health and social care services: the role of professional culture, *British Journal of Social Work*, 36:657–669.

Aries, P. (1962) *Centuries of Childhood*. London: Penguin.

Baldwin, M. (2001) Working together. Learning together: co-operative enquiry in the development of complex practice by teams of social workers. In Reason, P. and Bradbury, H. (eds), *Handbook of Action Research: Participation, Enquiry and Practice*. London: Sage, 179–188.

Balloch, S., Pahl, J. and McLean, J. (1988) Working in the social services: job satisfaction, stress and violence, *British Journal of Social* Work, 28:329–50.

Beck, U. (1992) *Risk Society: Towards a New Modernity*. London: Sage.

Beckett, C., McKeigue, B. and Taylor, H. (2007) Coming to conclusions: Social workers' perceptions of the decision-making process in care proceedings, *Child and Family Social Work*, 12:54–63.

Bee, H. (1997) *The Developing Child* (8th ed). New York: Longman.

Bee, H., & Boyd, D. (2006), *The Developing Child*. London: Pearson

Bell, M. (2002) Promoting children's rights through the use of relationship, *Child and Family Social Work*, 7(1):1–11.

Bennett, B. (2000) Self-managed learning and continuing professional development. In Cunningham, I., Bennett, B. and Dawes, D. (eds), *Self Managed Learning in Action: Putting SML into Practice*. Aldershot: Gower, 167–181.

Blewett, J., Lewis, J. and Tunstill, J. (2007) *The Changing Roles and Tasks of Social Work: A Literature Informed Discussion Paper*. London: GSCC.

Blom-Cooper, L., Harding, J. and Milton, E. (1987) *A Child in Mind*. London: Borough of Greenwich.

Boe, S. (1996) The experiences of students and practice teachers: Factors influencing students' practice learning. In Doel, M. and Shardlow, S. (eds), *Social Work in a Changing World: An International Perspective on Practice Learning*. Aldershot: Arena 117–131.

Bogo, M. (1996) Training, education and networking for practice teacher. In Doel, M. and Shardlow, S. (eds), *Social Work in a Changing World: An International Perspective on Practice Learning*. Aldershot: Arena 103–117.

Boud, D., Keogh, R. and Walker, D. (1985) *Reflection: Turning Experience into Learning*. London: Kogan Paul.

Bower, M. (2003) Broken and twisted, *Journal of Social Work Practice*, 17:143–153.

Bower, M. (2005) Psychoanalytic theories for social work practice. In Bower, M. (ed), *Psycho-analytic Theory for Social Work: Thinking under Fire*. London: Routledge, 3–14.

Bowlby, J. (1988) *A Secure Base: Clinical Applications of Attachment Theory.* London: Routledge.

Brandon, M., Schofield, G. and Trinder, L. (1998) *Social Work with Children.* Basingstoke: Macmillan.

Brearley, P.C. (1982) *Risk in Social Work.* London: Routledge & Kogan Paul.

Bridge, G. (1999) Child observation as a training strategy: Social work with disabled children and their families, *The International Journal of Infant Observation*, 2(2):51–66.

Bridge, G. and Miles, G. (eds) (1996) *On the Outside Looking In: Collected Essays in Young Child Observation in Social Work Training.* London: CCETSW.

Briggs, S. (1992) Child observation and social work training, *Journal of Social Work Practice*, 6(1):49–61.

Bronfenbrenner U. (1979) *The Ecology of Human Behaviour.* Cambridge: Harvard University Press.

Brown, A. and Bourne, I. (1996) *The Social Work Supervisor.* Open University Press.

Brown, K., and Keen, S. (2004) Post-qualifying awards in social work (Part 1): Necessary evil or panacea? *Social Work Education*, 23(1):77–92.

Bush, P. (ed) (1996) *Children, Medicines and Culture.* New York: Haworth Press.

Calder, M. (2004) Out of the frying pan into the fire? A critical analysis of the Integrated Children's System, *Child Care In Practice*, 10; 3:225–240.

Calder, M.C. and Hackett, S. (eds) (2003) *Assessment in Child Care – Using and Developing Frameworks.* Lyme Regis: Russell House Publishing.

Carroll, J. (1998) *Introduction to Therapeutic Play.* Oxford: Blackwell Science.

Caulkin, S. (2006) Are the real pros being managed out of existence? *Guardian*, 2 July.

Cecchin, C. (1987) Hypothesising, circularity and neutrality revisited: An invitation to curiousity, *Family Process*, 26:405–413.

Charles, M. (2004) Creativity and Constraint in Child Welfare. In Lymbery, M. and Butler, S. (eds), *Social Work Ideals and Practice Realities.* Basingstoke: Palgrave Macmillan, 179–199.

Clarke, J. (1998) Thriving on chaos? Managerialism and social welfare. In Carter, J. (ed), *Post Modernity and the Fragmentation of Welfare.* London: Routledge, pp. 171–186.

Collings, J. and Murray, P. (1996) Predictors of stress amongst social workers: An empirical study, *British Journal of Social Work*, 26:375–388.

Connelly, M. (1994), An act of empowerment: the Children and Young Person's and their Families Act, 1989, *British Journal of Social Work*, 24, pp. 87–100.

Cooper, A. (2004) Risk and The New Assessment Framework. In Calder, M. (ed), *Assessment for Childcare: Using and Developing Frameworks for Practice.* Lyme Regis: Russell House Publishing, pp. 100–120.

Cooper, A. (2005) Surface and depth in the Victoria Climbié inquiry report, *Child and Family Social Work*, 10(1):1–11.

Cooper, H., Braye, S. and Geyer, R. (2004) Complexity and inter-professional education, *Learning in Health and Social Care*, 3(4):179–189.

Corning, P. (1996) The co-operative gene: On the role of synergy in evolution, *Evolutionary Theory*, 11:183–207.

Coulshed, V. and Orme, J. (2006) *Social Work Practice.* Basingstoke: Palgrave Macmillan.

Coyne, J. A. and Holroyd, K. (1982) Stress, coping and illness: a transactional perspective, in EDS. T. Millon, C. Green & R Meagher, Handbook of Clinical Health Psychology, New York: Plenum, pp 103–127.

Cree, V. (2004) *Sociology for Social Workers and Probation Officers.* London: Routledge.

Cree, V. and Davis, A. (2007) *Voices from the Inside.* London: Routledge.

Cunningham, I., Bennett, B. and Dawes, D. (eds) (2000) *Self Managed Learning in Action: Putting SML into Practice.* Aldershot: Gower.

Dalgeish, L. I. (2004) Risks needs and consequences. In Calder, M. (ed), *Assessment for Childcare: Using and Developing Frameworks for Practice.* Lyme Regis: Russell House Publishing, pp. 86–99.

Dallos, R. and Draper, R. (2000) *Introduction to Family Therapy: Systemic Theory and Practice.* Buckingham: Open University Press.

Daniel, B. and Wassell, S. (2002) *The Early Years. Assessing and Promoting Resilience in Vulnerable Children 1.* Philadelphia: Jessica Kingsley.

Daniel, B. and Wassell, S. (2002) *Adolescence. Assessing and Promoting Resilience in Vulnerable Children 3.* Philadelphia: Jessica Kingsley.

Dawes, G. (2000) Self managed learning and qualification programmes. In Cunningham, I., Bennett, B. and Dawes, D. (eds), *Self Managed Learning in Action: Putting SML into Practice.* Aldershot: Gower, 167–181.

Dean, H. (2004) The implication of the third way social policy for inequality, social care and citizenship. In Lewis, J. and Surender, R. (eds), *Welfare State Change: Towards a Third Way?* Oxford: Oxford University Press.

De Boer, C. and Coady, N. (2007) Good helping relationships in child welfare: learning from stories of success, *Children and Family Social Work*, 12:32–42.

Department for Education and Skills (2004) *Every Child Matters: Change for Children.* London: HMSO.

Department for Education and Skills (2004) *Every Child Matters: Next Steps* (DfES, March 2004) available from DfES Publications, PO Box 5050, Sherwood Park, Annesley, Nottingham NG15 0DJ tel(0845 6022260) Ref DfES/0240/2004.

Department of Health (1995) *Child Protection: Messages from Research.* London: HMSO.

Department of Health (1996) Report to the DoH: Evaluation of the Family Support Initiative, Warren C.

Department of Health (1998) *Modernising Social Servi*ces. London: HMSO.

Department of Health (1998) *Quality Protects: Framework for Action.* London: HMSO.

Department of Health (2000) *Framework for the Assessment of Children in Need and their Families.* London: HMSO.

Department of Health (2002) *Rules and Requirements of Social Work.* London: HMSO.

Department of Health (2003) *The Victoria Climbié Inquiry: Report of An Inquiry.* London: HMSO.

Department of Health (2004) *National Service Framework for Children, Young People and Maternity Services*, London: HMSO.

Dobbs, D. (2006) A revealing reflection, *Scientific American Mind*, April/May: 22–27.

Doel, M. and Shardlow, S.M. (2005) *Modern Social Work Practice: Teaching and Learning in Practice Settings.* Aldershot: Ashgate.

Doel, M. and Shardlow, S. (eds) (1996) *Social Work in a Changing World: An International Perspective on Practice Learning.* Aldershot: Arena.

Doel, M., Sawdon, C., and Morrison, D. (eds) (2002) *Learning, Practice and Assessment – Signposting the Portfolio*, London: Jessica Kingsley.

Dominelli, L. (2004) *Social Work: Theory and Practice for a Changing Profession.* Cambridge: Polity Press.

Dominelli, L. (2002) Values in social work: Contested entities and enduring qualities. In Adams, R., Dominelli, L. and Payne, M. (eds), *Critical Practice in Social Work.* Basingstoke: Palgrave Macmillan.

Duhl, F., Kantor, D. and Duhl, B. (1973) Learning, space and action in family therapy: A primer of sculpture. In Bloch, D. (ed), *Techniques in Family Psychotherapy.* New York: Grune and Stratton.

Eby, M. (2000). Understanding Professional Development In Brechin, A., Brown, H. and Eby, M. (eds) *Critical Practice in Health and Social Care.* London: Sage.

Ellis, L., Lasson, I. and Solomon, R. (1998) *Keeping Children in Mind: A Model of Child Observation Practice.* London: CCETSW.

Eraut, M. (1995) Schon shock: A case for reframing reflection in action. *Teacher and Teaching: Theory and Practice*, 1(2):9–21.

Farmacopoulou, N. (2002) What lies underneath: An inter-organisational analysis of collaboration between education and social work, *British Journal of Social Work*, 32:1051–1066.

Fawcett, M. (1996) *Learning through Child Observation.* London: Jessica Kingsley.

Ferguson, H. (2005) Working with violence, the emotions and psychosocial dynamics of child protection: Reflections on the Victoria Climbié case, *Journal of Social Work Education*, 24(7):781–795.

Fisher, M., *et al.* (1986), *In and Out of Care*. London: BAAF

Fisher, T. and Somerton, J. (2000) Reflection on action: The process of helping social work students to develop their use of theory in practice, *Social Work Education*, 19(3):387–401.

Fonagy, P., Steele, M., Steele, H., Higgit, A. and Target, M. (1994) The Emanuel Miller memorial lecture 1992. The theory and practice of resilience, *Journal of Child Psychology*, 35(2):231–257.

Fook, J. (2002) *Social Work: Critical Theory and Practice*. London: Sage.

Foucault (1998) *The History of Sexuality (Vol 1): The Will of Knowledge*. London: Penguin.

Furniss, T. (1991) *The Multi-professional Handbook of Child Sexual Abuse: Integrated Management, Therapy and Legal Intervention*. London: Routledge.

Gardner, R. (2003) Working together to improve children's life chances: the challenge of inter-agency collaboration. In Weinstein, J., Whittington, C. and Leiba, T. (eds), *Collaboration in Social Work Practice*. London: Jessica Kingsley.

Garmezy, N. (1985) Stress-resistant children: The search for protective factors. In Rutter, M. (ed), (2000) *Resilience Reconsidered: Conceptual Considerations, Empirical Findings and Policy Implications*. In Shonkoff, J.P. and Meisels, S.J. (eds), *Handbook of Early Childhood Intervention* (2nd edn.). Cambridge: Cambridge University Press.

Garrett, P.M. (2003) *Remaking Social Work with Children and Families – A Critical Discussion on the Modernisation of Social Care*. London: Routledge.

Geddes, M. and Medway, J. (1977) The symbolic drawing of the family life space, *Family Process*, 16(2): 219–224.

General Social Care Council (2001) *Social Work Education Post-qualifying Training Handbook*, http://www.gscc.org.uk [accessed 23/09/06].

General Social Care Council (2002) *Guidance on the Assessment of Practice in the Workplace*. London: GSCC.

General Social Care Council (2002) *National Occupational Standards for Social Work*. London: GSCC.

General Social Care Council (2003) *Social Work Post-qualifying Framework: Response to Consultation*, http://www.gscc.org.uk [accessed 23/09/06].

General Social Care Council (2005) *Post-qualifying Framework for Social Work Education* http://www.gscc.org.uk [accessed 23/09/06].

General Social Care Council (2005) *Specialist Standards and Requirements for Post-qualifying Social Work Education and Training: Children and Young People, their Families and Carers*. London: GSCC.

General Social Care Council (2005) *Specialist Standards and Requirements for Post-qualifying Social Work Education and Training: Leadership and Management*. London: GSCC.

General Social Care Council (2006) *Specialist Standards and Requirements for Post-qualifying Social Work Education and Training: Practice Education*. London: GSCC.

General Social Care Council (2007) *GSCC PQ Framework: Guidance for Enabling Others Requirement at Specialist Level*. London: GSCC.

Gerhardt, S. (2004) *Why Love Matters*. London: Routledge.

Germain, C. (1991) *Human Behaviour in the Social Environment*. New York: Columbia University Press.

Germain, C. and Bloom, M. (1999) *Human Behaviour in the Social Environment: An Ecological View*. New York: Columbia University Press.

Gilligan, R. (2001) Promoting positive outcomes for children in need: The assessment of protective factors. In Horwath, J. (ed), *The Child's World*. London: Jessica Kingsley, 180–193.

Goleman, D. (1996) *Emotional Intelligence: Why it Can Matter More than IQ*. London: Bloomsbury.

Gould, N. (1996) Introduction: Social work education and the crisis of the professions. In Gould, N. and Taylor, I. (eds), *Reflective Learning for Social Work*. Aldershot: Arena, 1–10.

Gupta, A. and Blewett, J. (2007) Change for children? The challenges and opportunities for children's social workforce, *Child and Family Social Work*, 12:172–181.

Gurney, H. (2000) Risk management. In Davies, M. (ed), *The Blackwell Encyclopaedia of Social Work.* Oxford: Blackwell, pp. 123–130.

Haigh, R. (1999) The quintessence of a therapeutic environment – Five universal qualities. In Campling, P. and Haigh, R. (eds), *Therapeutic Communities: Past, Present and Future.* London: Jessica Kingsley, 246–257.

Halmos, P. (1995) *The Faith of the Counsellors.* London: Constable.

Halpern, R. (1988) *Parent Support and Education for Low-income Families: Historical and Current Perspectives.* Chicago: Reprints from Erikson Institute.

Halpern, R. (1988), Parent support and education for low-income families: historical and current perspectives, *Children and Youth Services Rewiew*, Vol. 10, No. 4, 283–303.

Hanko, G. (1999) *Increasing Competence through Collaborative Problem Solving – Using Insight into Social and Emotional Factors in Children's Learning.* London: David Fulton Publishers.

Harm, T. and van der Westhuizen, G. (2006) Knowledge construction in collaborative enquiry among teachers, *Teachers and Teaching: Theory and Practice*, 12(1):51–67.

Harrison, K. and Ruch, G. (2007) Social work and the use of self: On becoming and being a social worker. In Lymbery, M. and Postle, K. (eds), *Social Work: A Companion to Learning.* London: Sage, 40–50.

Healy, K. (2001) Participatory action research and social work – a critical appraisal, *International Social Work*, 44 (1):93–105.

Heap, R. (2005) Happy in their work, *Community* Care, May:34–35.

Hedges, F. (2005) *An Introduction to Systemic Therapy with Families.* Basingstoke: Palgrave Macmillan.

Hendrick, H. (2003) *Child Welfare: Historical Dimensions, Contemporary Debate.* Bristol: Policy Press.

Her Majesty's Treasury (2004) *The National Childcare Strategy.* London: HMSO.

Heron, J. and Reason, P. (2001). The practice of co-operative inquiry: Research 'with' rather than 'on' people. In Reason, P. and Bradbury, H. (eds), *Handbook of Action Research: Participation, Enquiry and Practice.* London: Sage, 179–188.

Hess, P., McGowan, B. and Botsko, M. (2003) *Nurturing the One, Supporting the Many.* New York: Columbia University Press.

Higham, P. (2006) *Social Work: Introducing Professional Practice.* London: Sage Publications.

Hill, M., & Tisdall, K. (1997), *Children and Society.* Harlow: Longman.

Hirsch, B.J. (1981) Social networks and the coping process: Creating personal communities. In Gottlieb, B.H. (ed), *Social Networks and Social Support.* Beverley Hills, CA: Sage, 149–170.

HMSO (1946) *Report of the Care of Children Committee.* (The Curtis Report), Cmnd 6922, London: HMSO.

HMSO (2004) *The Children Act 2004.* London: HMSO.

Hood, C., Rothstein, H. and Baldwin, R. (2001) *The Government of Risk: Understanding Risk Regulation Regimes.* Oxford: Oxford University Press.

Holmes, J. (1993) *John Bowlby and Attachment Theory (Makers of Modern Psychotherapy).* London: Routledge.

Horwath, J. (2001), *The Child's World: Assessing Children in Need* . London: Jessica Kingsley

Howe, D. (1987) *An Introduction to Social Work Theory.* Aldershot: Wildewood House.

Howe, D. (1995) *Attachment Theory for Social Work Practice.* London: Macmillan.

Howe, D., Brandon, M., Hinings, D. and Schofield, G. (1999) *Attachment Theory, Child Maltreatment and Family Support.* London: Palgrave.

Hughes, L. and Heycox, K. (1996) Three perspectives on assessment in practice learning. In Doel, M. and Shardlow, S. (eds), *Social Work in a Changing World.* Aldershot: Arena.

Hughes, L. and Pengelly, P. (1997) *Staff Supervision in a Turbulent Environment: Managing Process and Task in Frontline Services.* London: Jessica Kingsley.

Hugman, R. (2005) *New Approaches in Ethics for the Caring Professions.* Basingstoke: Palgrave/Macmillan.

Humphries, B. (1988) Adult learning in social work education: Towards liberation or domestication, *Journal of Critical Social Policy*, September; 8:4–21.

Hunter, M. (2001) *Psychotherapy with Young People in Care*. East Sussex: Brunner-Routledge.

Huxham, C. (1993) Collaborative capability: An inter-organisational perspective on collaborative advantage, *Public Money and Management*, Autumn: 21–27.

Imber-Black, E. (1998) *Families and Wider Systems – A Family Therapist's Guide Through the Labyrinth*. New York: Guilford Press.

Ixer, G. (1999) There's no such thing as reflection, *British Journal of Social Work*, 29:513–527.

Ixer, G. (2000) Assumptions about reflective practice. In Harris, J., Froggett, L. and Paylor, I. (eds), *Reclaiming Social Work: The Southport Papers Volume One*. Birmingham: Venture Press, 79–92.

Jaeger, C., Renn, O., Rosa and Webler, T. (2001) *Risk, Uncertainty and Rational Action*. London: Earthscan Publications.

James, A., Jenks, C. and Proust, A. (1998), *Theorizing Childhood*. Cambridge: Polity Press.

Johns, C. (2004) *Becoming a Reflective Practitioner* 2nd edn. Oxford: Blackwell Publishing.

Jones, C. and Tucker, S. (2001) Voices from the front line: State social workers and New Labour, *British Journal of Social Work*, 31:547–62.

Jordan, B. (1987) Counselling, advocacy and negotiation, *British Journal of Social Work*, 17:135–146.

Jordan, B. (2000) *Social Work and the Third Way: Tough Love as Social Policy*. London: Sage.

Kadushin, A. (1976) *Supervision in Social Work*. Columbia University Press.

Kanter, J. (ed) (2005) *Face to Face with Children: The Life and Work of Clare Winnicott*. London: Karnac.

Kemshall, H. and Pritchard, J. (eds) (1997) *Good Practice in Risk Assessment and Management: Volume – 2 Protection, Rights and Responsibilities*. London: Jessica Kingsley.

Kilkey, M. (2006) New Labour and reconciling work and family life: Making it father's business, *Social Policy and Society*, 5:167–175.

King, R. (2002) Experience of undertaking infant observation as part of the post-qualifying award in child care, *Journal of Social Work Practice*, 6(2):213–22.

Kirkpatrick, I. (1999) The worst of both worlds? Public services without markets or bureaucracy, *Public Money and Management*, Oct–Dec:7–14.

Klaehn, R.L. and Martner, J. (2003) A conceptual framework for an early childhood system of care. In Punariega, A. and Winters, N. (eds), *Handbook of Child and Adolescent Systems of Care: The New Community Psychiatry*. New York: Jossey-Bass.

Klein, G. (1998) *Sources of Power: How People Make Decisions*. MIT.

Korbin, J. (1997), Culture and child maltreatment. In Helfer, M., Kempe, R. and Krugman, R.D. (eds), *The Battered Child*. London: University of Chicago Press.

Lambert, C. (2001) *Promoting resilience in 'looked after children'*. University of East Anglia: Social Work Monographs.

Langley, S. (2006) *A Study that Examines Children and Families Social Workers' Experiences of Supervision within Hampshire County Council'*, Unpublished MA Dissertation in Advanced Social Work Studies: Reading University.

Laybourn, A., Brown, J. and Hill, M. (2002) *Hurting on the Inside*. Aldershot: Avebury Ashgate.

Le Grand, J. (2006) *Motivation, Agency and Public Policy: Of Knights and Knaves, Pawns and Queens*. Oxford: Oxford University Press. (Revised Paperback Edition.)

Le Riche, P. and Tanner, K. (eds) (1998) *Observation and its Application to Social Work: Rather Like Breathing*. London: Jessica Kingsley.

Lewis, J. and Surender, R. (2004) *Welfare State Change: Towards a Third Way?* Oxford: Oxford University Press.

Lightburn, A. and Sessions, P. (2005) *Community-based Clinical Practice*. New York: Oxford University Press.

Lishman, J. (1994) *Handbook of Theory for Practice Teachers in Social Work*. Jessica Kingsley.

Lister R. (2003) Investing in the citizen-workers of the future: transformations in citizenship and the state under New Labour, *Social Policy and Administration*, Vol. 37, No. 5, October.

Lister, R. (2004) The Third Way's social investment state. In Lewis, J. and Surender, R. (eds), *Welfare State Change: Towards a Third Way?* Oxford: Oxford University Press.

London Borough of Brent (1985) *A Child in Trust: The Report into the Inquiry Into the Case of Jasmine Beckford.* London: HMSO.

Looi Chng, V. and Coombs, S. (2004) Applying self-organised learning to develop critical thinkers for learning organisations: A conversational action research project, *Educational Action Research*, 12(3):363–386.

Lupton, D. (1999) *Risk.* London: Routledge.

Lymbery, M. and Butler, S. (eds) (2004) *Social Work Ideals and Practice Realities.* Basingstoke: Palgrave Macmillan.

Macdonald, K.I. and Macdonald, G.M. (1999) Perceptions of risk. In Parsloe, P. (ed), *Risk Assessment in Social Care and Social Work. Research Highlights in Social Work No. 36.* London: Jessica Kingsley.

Martyn, H. (2000) Introduction. In Martyn, H. (ed), *Developing Reflective Practice in a World of Change.* Bristol: Polity Press, 2–9.

Maythen, G. (2004) *Ulrich Beck.* London: Pluto Press.

McMahon, L. and Farnfield, S. (1994) Infant and child observation as preparation for social work practice, *Social Work Education*, 13(3):81–98.

Mattinson, J. (1992) *The Reflective Process in Social Work Supervision* (2nd edn). London: The Tavistock Institute of Marital Studies.

McDonald, C., Harris, J. and Wintersteen, R. (2003) Contingent on context? Social work and the state in Australia, Britain and the USA, *British Journal of Social Work*, 33(2):191–208.

Menzies, I. (1970) *The Functioning of Social Systems as a Defence Against Anxiety.* London: Tavistock Institute.

Menzies-Lyth, I. (1988) *Containing Anxiety in Institutions: Selected Essays Volume One.* London: Free Association Books.

Menzies-Lyth, I. (1989) *The Dynamics of the Social.* London: Free Association Books.

Mezirow, J. (1981) A critical theory of adult learning and education, *Journal of Adult Education*, 32(1):3–24.

Miles, G. (2004) Commentary (12 years on) on 'The contribution of child observation training to professional development in social work' by Judith Trowell and Gillian Miles, *Journal of Social Work Practice*, 18(1):61–64.

Miller, M., Rustin, M., Rustin., M. and Shuttleworth, J. (eds) (1989) *Closely Observed Infants.* London: Duckworth.

Mitchell, C. (2001) Partnership for continuing professional development: The impact of the post-qualifying award for social workers (PQSW) on social work practice, *Social Work Education*, 20(4):433–445.

Moffat, K., George, U., Lee, B. and McGrath, S. (2005) Community practice researchers as reflective learners, *British Journal of Social Work*, 35(1):89–14.

Morgan, J., Rawlinson, M. and Weaver, M. (2006) Facilitating on-line reflective learning for health and social care professionals, *Open Learning*, 21(2):167–176.

Morgan, R. (2006) *About Social Workers: A Childrens' Views Report.* London: Commission for Social Care Inspection.

Morrison, B. (1997) *What If?* London: Granta.

Morrison, T. (1996) *Staff Supervision in Social Care: An Action Learning Approach.* Brighton: Pavilion Publishing.

Morrison, T. (2007) Emotional intelligence, emotion and social work: Context, characteristics, complications and contribution, *British Journal of Social Work*, 37:245–263.

Mulcahy, G. (2000) Putting modernisation into practice, *Journal of Professional Social Work*, April:10–11.

Munro, E. (2001) Empowering looked after children, *Child and Family Social Work*, 6(2):129–137.

Munro, E. (2004) The impact of audit on social work practice, *British Journal of Social Work*, 34:1077–1097.

Murphy, M. (2004) *Developing Collaborative Relationships in Inter-agency Child Protection.* Lyme Regis: Russell House.

Nixon, P. (2001) An introduction to family group conferences. In Cull, L. and Roche, J. (eds), *The Law and Social Work – Contemporary Issues for Social Work.* Basingstoke: Palgrave.

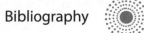

Norris, D. (1990) *Violence Against Social Workers – the implications for practice*, London: Jessica Kingsley.

Novotny, C. (2005) The increase of complexity and reduction – Emergent interfaces between the natural sciences, humanities, and social sciences, *Theory, Culture and Society*, 22(5):15–31.

Oaklander, V. (1978) *Windows to Our Children*. New York: Real People Press.

O'Hagan, K. (1997) *Competence in Social Work Practice*. Jessica Kingsley.

Olney, F. (2001) Management in supervision and practice, *Journal of Professional Social Work*, May:10–11.

Orme, N. (2003) *Medieval Children*. New York: Yale University Press.

Papp, P., Silverstein, O. and Carter, E. (1973) Family sculpting in preventative work with 'well families', *Family Process*, 12:197–212.

Parker, J. and Bradley, G. (2003) *Social Work Practice, Assessment, Planning, Intervention and Review*, Learning Matters.

Parsloe, P. (ed) (1999) *Risk Assessment in Social Care and Social Work*.

Parton, N. (2006) *Safeguarding Childhood: Early Intervention and Surveillance in a Late Modern Society*. Basingstoke: Palgrave Macmillan.

Parton, N. (1998) Risk, advanced liberalism and child welfare: The need to rediscover uncertainty, *British Journal of Social Work*, 28:5–27.

Parton, N. (ed) (1996) *Social Theory, Social Change and Social Work*. London: Routledge.

Peberdy, A. (1993) Observing. In Shakespeare, P., Atkinson, D. and French, S. (eds), *Reflecting in Research Practice. Issues in Health and Social Welfare*. Buckingham: Open University Press, 47–57.

Pietroni-Miller, M. (1998) Beyond the bureau-professional. In Le Riche, P. and Tanner, K. (eds), *Observation and its Application to Social Work: Rather Like Breathing*. London: Jessica Kingsley, 111–142.

Postle, K., Edwards, C., Moon, R., Rumsey, H. and Thomas, T. (2002) Continuing professional development after qualification – Partnerships, potential and pitfalls, *Social Work Education*, 21(2):157–169.

Practice Learning Taskforce (2006) *Induction to Work-based Learning*. London: Department of Health/Skills for Care.

Prince, K. (2003) *Boring Records*. Lyme Regis: Russell House Publishing.

Reder, P. and Duncan, S. (2004) Making the most of the Victoria Climbié report, *Child Abuse Review*, 13:95–114.

Reimers, S. and Treacher, A. (1995) *Introducing User-friendly Family Therapy*. London: Routledge.

Ridley, M. (2003), *Nature via Nurture*. London: Harper Perennial.

Rolfe, G., Freshwater, D. and Jasper, M. (2001) *Critical Reflection for Nursing and the Helping Professions: A User's Guide*. Basingstoke: Palgrave.

Rossi, P. H., Schuerman, J. and Budde, P. (1996) *Understanding Child Maltreatment Decisions and Those that Make Them*. Chicago: University of Chicago, Chapin Hall Centre for Children.

Rousseau, J. (1993) *Emile*. London: Phoenix.

Ruch, G. (2002) From triangle to spiral: Reflective practice in social work education, *Practice and Research in Social Work Education*, 21(2):199–216.

Ruch, G. (2004) *Reflective Practice in Contemporary Child Care Social Work*, Unpublished PhD thesis: University of Southampton.

Ruch, G. (2005) Relationship-based and reflective practice: Holistic approaches to contemporary child care social work, *Child and Family Social Work*, 10:111–123.

Ruch, G. (2007a) 'Thoughtful' practice in child care social work: The role of case discussion, *Child and Family Social Work*, 12(4):???

Ruch, G. (2007b) Reflective practice in child care social work: The role of containment, *British Journal of Social Work*, 37:659–680.

Ruch, G. (2007c). 'Knowing', mirroring and containing: Experiences of facilitating child observation seminars on a post-qualification child care programme, *Social Work Education*, 26(2):169–184.

Rustin, M. (1989) Encountering primitive anxieties. In Miller, L., Rustin, M., Rustin, M. and Shuttleworth, J. (eds), *Closely Observed Infants*. London: Duckworth, 7–21.

Rustin, M. (2004) Learning from the Victoria Climbié Enquiry, *Journal of Social Work Practice*, 18(1):9–18.

Rustin, M. (2005) Conceptual analysis of critical moments in the life of Victoria Climbié, *Child and Family Social Work*, 10(1):11–19.

Rutter, L. (2006) Skills support for post-qualifying education: Tailoring programmes to meet students' needs, *Social Work Education*, 25(3):279–287.

Rutter, M. (2000) Resilience reconsidered: Conceptual considerations, empirical findings and policy implications. In Shonkoff, J.P. and Meisels, S.J. (eds), *Handbook of Early Childhood Intervention* (2nd edn). Cambridge University Press.

Saleeby, D. (2001) *Human Behavior and Social Environments: A Bio-psychosocial Approach*. New York: Columbia University Press.

Schon, D. (1983) *The Reflective Practitioner*. New York: Basic Books.

Schon, D. (1987) *Educating the Reflective Practitioner*. San Francisco: Jossey-Bass.

SCIE (2003) *Users at the heart – user participation in the governance and operations of social care regulatory bodies*, SCIE Report No. 5. London: SCIE.

SCIE (2004), *Involving service users and carers in social work education*, Resource Guide No. 2., London: SCIE.

Service User Inclusion Group (SUIG) *Notes from a Creativity Workshop*. Unpublished document, University of Portsmouth.

Sharp, M. and Danbury, H. (1999) *The Management of Failing DipSW Students*, Ashgate.

Sheldon, B. and Chilvers, R. (2005) *Evidenced-based Social Care*. Lyme Regis: Russell House Publishing.

Sheppard, M. (1995) Social work, social science and practice wisdom, *British Journal of Social Work*, 25: 265–293.

Shilling, C. (2003) *The Body and Social Theory*. London: Sage.

Shonkoff, J. and Phillips, D. (2007) From Neurons to Neighbourhood, Report from the National Research Council and Institute of Medicine, 500 Fifth St. N.W. Washington D.C., 20001, USA.

Shore, A. (2001) The effects of early relational trauma on right brain development, affect regulation, and infant mental health, *Infant Mental Health Journal*, 22(1–2):201–269.

Shuttleworth, J. (1991) Psychoanalytic theory and infant development. In Miller, L., Rustin, M., Rustin, M. and Shuttleworth, J. (eds), *Closely Observed Infants*. London: Duckworth, 22–51.

Simmonds, J. (1998) Observing the unthinkable in residential care. In Le Riche, P. and Tanner, K. (eds), *Observation and its Application to Social Work: Rather Like Breathing*. London: Jessica Kingsley, 91–110.

Simmonds, J. (1988) Introduction. In Aldgate, J. and Simmonds, J. (eds), *Direct Work with Children: A Guide for Social Work Practitioners*. London: Batsford/BAAF, 1–21.

Singh, G. (2006) *Developing and supporting black and minority ethnic practice teachers and assessors*. London: Practice Learning Taskforce, Department of Health/Skills for Care.

Singh, R.R. (1996) Developing practice learning at a school of social work: Process, perspectives and outcome. In Doel, M. and Shardlow, S. (eds), *Social Work in a Changing World: An International Perspective on Practice Learning*. Aldershot: Arena.

Smith, M. (2000) Supervision of fear in social work: A re-evaluation of reassurance, *Journal of Social Work Practice*, 14(1):17–26.

Smith, M. (2005) *Surviving Fears in Health and Social Care – The Terrors of Night and the Arrows of Day*. London: Jessica Kingsley.

Skinner, K. and Whyte, B. (2004) Going beyond training: Theory and practice in managing learning, *Social Work Education*, 23(4):365–381.

Snowden, D.J. (2003) Managing for serendipity, ARK Knowledge, Management, Vol 6, Issue 8.

Sobiechawska, P. and Maisch, M. (2006) Work-based learning: In search of an effective model, *Educational Action Research*, 14(2):267–286.

Stalker, K. (2003) Managing risk and uncertainty in social work, *British Journal of Social Work*, 32:211–233.

Statham, D. (2004) Research and the management of practice. In Statham, D. (ed), *Managing Frontline Practice in Social Care*. London: Jessica Kingsley, 157–166.

Steele, L. (1998) Keeping a precarious balance, *Community Care*, 10–16 September

Stepney, P. (2000) The theory to practice debate revisited. In Stepney, P. and Ford, D. (eds), *Social Work Models, Methods and Theories*. Lyme Regis: Russell House Publishing.

Stevenson, O. (2005) Guest Editor, Special issue: Interdisciplinary working in child welfare, *Child and Family Social Work*, 10(3):

Stevenson, O. (2005) Genericism and specialization: The story since 1970, *British Journal of Social Work*, 35:569–586.

Stevenson, O. (2005) Foreword. In Bower, M. (ed), *Psycho-analytic Theory for Social Work: Thinking under Fire*. London: Routledge, ix–xvi.

Stroul B. (ed) (1996) *Children's Mental Health*. Baltimore: Paul Brookes.

Sugarman, L. (1986) *Lifespan Development Concepts, Theories and Interventions*. London: Routledge.

Taylor, H., Beckett, C. and Mc-Keigue, B. (2008) 'Judgements of Solomon: Anxiety and Defences of Social Workers in Care Proceedings', *Child and Family Social Work*, 13, pp.23–31.

Thoburn, J., Lewis, A. and Shemmings, D. (1995) *Paternalism or Partnership? Family Involvement in the Child Protection Process*. London: HMSO.

Thompson, K. (2002) *Moral Panics*. London: Routledge.

Thompson, N. (2006) *Anti-discriminatory Practice*. Basingstoke: Palgrave Macmillan.

Thompson, N. (2002) *Building the Future, Social Work with Children, Young People and their Families*. Lyme Regis: Russell House Publishing.

Thompson, N. (1995) *Theory and Practice in Health and Social Welfare* Buckingham: Open University Press.

Tosey, P. (2002) *Teaching on the edge of chaos. Complexity theory and teaching systems*. LTSN Imaginative Curriculum Development Paper. URL: http://www.ltsn.ac.uk

Training Organisation of Personal Social Services (2002) *The National Occupational Standards*. TOPSS.

Trowell, J. (1995) Key psychoanalytic concepts. In Trowell, J. and Bower, M. (eds), *The Emotional Needs of Young Children and Their Families: Using Psycho-analytic Ideas in the Community*. London: Routledge, 12–21.

Trowell, J. and Miles, G. (1991) The contribution of observation training to professional development in social work, *Journal of Social Work Practice*, 5(1):51–60.

Tunstill, J., Meadows, P., Allnock, D., Akhurst, S., Chrysanthou, J., Garbers, C., Morley, A. and Van de Velde, T. (2005) *Implementing Sure Start Local Programmes: An In-depth Study*. London: DfES.

Van Den, Berg, J. and Grealish, E. (1986) Individualised services and supports through the wraparound process: Philosophy and procedures, *Journal of Child and Family Studies*, 5:7–21.

van der Veer, R. and Valsiner, J. (1994) *The Vygotsky Reader*. London: Blackwell.

Warren-Adamson, C. (ed) (2002) *Family Centres and their International Role in Social Action*. Aldershot: Ashgate.

Warren-Adamson, C. (2005) Reflections on partnership practice and children and young people who are looked after. In Wheal, A. (ed), *Companion to Foster Care*. Lyme Regis: Russell House Publishing, 40–48.

Warren-Adamson, C. and Lightburn, A. (2006) Developing a community-based model for integrated family centre practice. In Lightburn, A. and Sessions, P. (eds), *Handbook of Community-based Clinical Practice*. Oxford: Oxford University Press.

Warren-Adamson, C. (2007) Collaborative enquiry and its potential in practice research: exploring kinship care, SPRING Occasional Paper, Division of Social Work, University of Southampton, UK.

Watzlawick, P., Weakland, J. & Fisch, R. (1974), *Change – Principles of Problem Formation and Problem Resolution*, New York and London: Norton.

Webb, A. (2006) *Social Work in a Risk Society*. Basingstoke: Palgrave.

Webb, S. (2001) Some considerations on the validity of evidenced-based practice, *British Journal of Social Work*, 31:57–59.

Werner, E.E. (2000) *Protective factors and individual resilience*. In Shonkoff, J.P. and Meisels, S.J. (eds), *Handbook of Early Childhood Intervention* (2nd edn). Cambridge University Press.

Whittaker, J. (1986) Integrating formal and informal social care: A conceptual framework, *British Journal of Social Work*, 16; Supplement:39–62.

Whittaker, J.K., Schinke S.P. and Gilchrist, L.D. (1986) The ecological paradigm in child, youth and family services: Implications for policy and practice, *Social Service Review*, December: 483–583.

Whyte, D. (2002) *The Heart Aroused – Poetry and the Preservation of the Soul in Corporate America*. New York: Currency Books.

Williams, B. (2001) The theoretical links between problem-based learning and self-directed learning for continuing professional nursing education, *Teaching in Higher Education*, 6(1):85–98.

Williams, F. (2004) What matters is who works: Why every child matters to New Labour: Commentary on the Dfes green paper Every Child Matters, *Critical Social Policy*, 24(3):406–427.

Wilson, K. (1992) The place of child observation in social work training, *Journal of Social Work Practice*, 6(1):37–47.

Winnicott, D.W. (1965), *The Maturational Process in the Facilitating Environment*, Karnac Books, London.

Woodcock, P. and Dixon, J. (2005) Professional ideologies and preferences in social work: A British study in global perspective, *British Journal of Social Work*, 35:953–973

Wolfensberger, W. (1977) *A Global Multi-Component Advocacy Protection Schema*, Monograph, Canadian Association for the Mentally Retarded, 4700, Keele Street, Downsview, Toronto, Ontario, Canada.

Index

168   Index